Outward Foreign Direct Investment and US Exports, Jobs, and R&D: Implications for US Policy

Gary Clyde Hufbauer, Theodore H. Moran, and Lindsay Oldenski, assisted by Martin Vieiro

FSC
www.fsc.org
MIX
Paper from
responsible sources
FSC® C005010

Outward Foreign Direct Investment and US Exports, Jobs, and R&D: Implications for US Policy

Gary Clyde Hufbauer, Theodore H. Moran, and Lindsay Oldenski, assisted by Martin Vieiro

PETERSON INSTITUTE FOR INTERNATIONAL ECONOMICS
Washington, DC
August 2013

Gary Clyde Hufbauer, Reginald Jones Senior Fellow since 1992, was formerly the Maurice Greenberg Chair and Director of Studies at the Council on Foreign Relations (1996–98); the Marcus Wallenberg Professor of International Finance Diplomacy at Georgetown University (1985–92); senior fellow at the Peterson Institute (1981–85); deputy director of the International Law Institute at Georgetown University (1979–81); deputy assistant secretary for international trade and investment policy of the US Treasury (1977–79); and director of the international tax staff at the Treasury (1974–76). Hufbauer is author, coauthor, or editor of numerous books on international trade, investment, and tax issues, including *Figuring Out the Doha Round* (2010), *US Taxation of Foreign Income* (2007), and *Reforming the US Corporate Tax* (2005).

Theodore H. Moran, nonresident senior fellow, has been associated with the Peterson Institute for International Economics since 1998. He holds the Marcus Wallenberg Chair at the School of Foreign Service in Georgetown University. He is the founder of the Landegger Program in International Business Diplomacy at the university and serves as director there. He is also a member of Huawei's International Advisory Council. Since 2007 he has served as associate to the US National Intelligence Council on international business issues. Moran has published numerous books on foreign direct investment, including *Foreign Direct Investment in the United States: Benefits, Suspicions, and Risks with Special Attention to FDI from China* (2013), *Foreign Direct Investment and Development* (2011), *Three Threats: An Analytical Framework for the CFIUS Process* (2009).

Lindsay Oldenski is assistant professor in the Landegger Program in International Business Diplomacy at Georgetown University's School of Foreign Service. Prior to joining the Georgetown faculty, she taught at the Johns Hopkins University School of Advanced International Studies and California State University, San Marcos. She was also an economist at the US Department of Treasury, an analyst at the Federal Reserve Bank of Boston, and a consultant in the biotech industry. Her research on international trade and multinational organizations

has been published in both academic journals and policy forums. She is coauthor of *Foreign Direct Investment in the United States: Benefits, Suspicions, and Risks with Special Attention to FDI from China* (2013).

PETERSON INSTITUTE FOR INTERNATIONAL ECONOMICS
1750 Massachusetts Avenue, NW
Washington, DC 20036-1903
(202) 328-9000   FAX: (202) 659-3225
www.piie.com

Adam S. Posen, *President*
Edward A. Tureen, *Director of Publications, Marketing, and Web Development*

Printing by Versa Press, Inc.

Printed in the United States of America
15 14 13   5 4 3 2 1

Library of Congress Cataloging-in-Publication Data
Hufbauer, Gary Clyde.
   Outward FDI, US exports, US jobs, and US R & D implications for US policy / Gary Clyde Hufbauer and Theodore H. Moran.
     pages cm
   Includes bibliographical references.
   ISBN 978-0-88132-668-0
   1. Investments, Foreign—United States. 2. International business enterprises—United States. 3. Research, Industrial—United States. 4. Economic development—United States. 5. United States—Economic policy—2009- I. Moran, Theodore H., 1943- II. Title.
   HG4910.H83 2013
   338.8'8973—dc23
                                  2012048605

This publication has been subjected to a prepublication peer review intended to ensure analytical quality. The views expressed are those of the authors. This publication is part of the overall program of the Peterson Institute for International Economics, as endorsed by its Board of Directors, but it does not necessarily reflect the views of individual members of the Board or of the Institute's staff or management. The Institute is an independent, private, nonprofit institution for rigorous, intellectually honest study and open discussion of international economic policy. Its work is made possible by financial support from a highly diverse group of philanthropic foundations, private corporations, and interested individuals, as well as by income on its capital fund. For a list of Institute supporters, please see www.piie.com/supporters.cfm.

Contents

Figures

Preface

Foreign direct investment (FDI) by US-based multinational corporations (MNCs) has become one the most potent drivers of global economic expansion in recent decades. The increasing globalization of US firms has contributed to US economic strength as well as the strength of the economies where their foreign subsidiaries and affiliates are located. Research by the Peterson Institute for International Economics and others has established that the plants of US MNCs are more productive and pay higher wages than domestic firms and are among the most important engines of jobs, especially in research and development (R&D).

But there is no question that the visible and large investment decisions of US MNCs nonetheless generate apprehension among many Americans. Recent political campaigns have been rife with charges that major multinationals are "shipping jobs" to low-wage or low-tax countries and contributing to the stagnation of the US economy after the Great Recession of 2008–09. More substantively, policymakers and elected officials are engaged in important debates about the merits of using tax policy, education and training, infrastructure investment, and other actions to encourage investment at home as opposed to overseas.

This study addresses with data one of the most widespread sources of concern, the actual consequences for the US economy as American MNCs spread technology and reposition production around the globe. Based on the observed behavior of some 1,500 US MNCs over two decades, the study traces how the home operations of US MNCs have changed as these firms have expanded or contracted their foreign operations. The authors—Gary Clyde Hufbauer, Theodore H. Moran, and Lindsay Oldenski, assisted by Martin Vieiro—analyze head-on the big question of test whether outward FDI by

US multinationals substitutes for economic activity in the United States or complements and strengthens their operations at home.

Using best current econometric techniques, the analysis presented in this volume demonstrates that increases in four types of activity (employment, sales, capital expenditures, and R&D) in US MNC affiliates abroad are all *positively* associated with growth in those same four activities in the United States plus exports. Across all fronts, the authors' analysis shows that an *increase* in outward FDI by a US company is associated with an increase in productive domestic US activities by that same firm.

Thus, on the basis of the analysis presented here, some widely discussed measures aimed at impeding US MNC expansion abroad will be counterproductive. Limiting or discouraging FDI by US MNCs will *weaken* job creation, investment, R&D, and exports at home, rather than strengthening or enhancing domestic economic activity. The authors argue that one such measure, imposing the same high corporate tax rate on overseas operations as the United States imposes on corporate earnings within the country, would be a particular mistake. This step would sharply disadvantage US MNCs relative to their peers based in Europe, Japan, and other economies. Over time, US MNCs would lose market share, and the US economy would suffer.

It is important to note that the findings reported in this study do not mean that there are only winners and no losers from contemporary shifts in trade and investment. Changing patterns of MNC activity—like changing patterns of business and technology more generally—generate job loss as well as creation, meaning dislocations for some workers as well as new opportunities for others. The changing pattern of production may, at the same time, shift relative demand for types of labor and thereby increase wage disparities between skilled and less skilled workers in the labor force.

The authors argue, however, that it would be self-defeating for the US economy to impede the search for efficiency gains and expanding markets by US-based multinationals. The appropriate response for the United States to job dislocation associated with multinational investment is the same as it is for trade, another aspect of globalization that has brought huge benefits but has undeniably hurt some specific communities and economic sectors. The US government should design and fund adjustment, retraining, and other compensatory programs to cushion the impact on those adversely affected. It should not impede capital flows in a futile effort to preserve jobs in uncompetitive home-country economic activities.

This volume on outward FDI from the United States is a sister study to *Foreign Direct Investment in the United States: Benefits, Suspicions, and Risks with Special Attention to FDI from China*, by Theodore Moran and Lindsay Oldenski, and comes to a common conclusion: The policy challenge with respect to FDI in the years ahead is to create a more favorable setting for multinational investors to locate their best jobs, most beneficial operations, and most dynamic activities here in the United States. To make the United States more competitive as a location for international business operations, the volume offers recommendations for upgrading infrastructure, reforming immigration, and making substantial improvements in education. The authors argue that most importantly the United States should sharply reduce its corporate tax rate and adopt a territorial tax system, as have the great majority of countries that compete with the United States in global markets.

These two volumes are results of the Peterson Institute's efforts to objectively analyze the impact of trade and investment on the United States and other economies and to prepare relevant practical policy responses to that impact. At a time when many public discussions of FDI are filled with emotional and misleading invocations of "economic patriotism" and "corporate responsibility," it is more important than ever to use fact-based econometric analysis of firm-level data to investigate the issues. This effort is all the more important now that the economic policy debate has gone far beyond traditional conceptions of comparative advantage in international trade to structural issues and investment flows. These two studies should be read in light of the recent Peterson Institute publications *Rising Tide: Is Growth in Emerging Economies Good for the United States?* by Lawrence Edwards and Robert Z. Lawrence and *Global Trade in Services: Fear, Facts, and Offshoring* by J. Bradford Jensen, which address related issues with similar business microdata driven approaches. Together, we believe that these studies provide a robust set of conclusions and policy recommendations that policymakers can use in the contemporary world of global supply chains.

The Peterson Institute for International Economics is a private, nonprofit institution for rigorous, intellectually open, and honest study and discussion of international economic policy. Its purpose is to identify and analyze important issues to making globalization beneficial and sustainable for the people of the United States and the world and then to develop and communicate practical new approaches for dealing with them. The Institute is completely nonpartisan.

The Institute's work is funded by a highly diverse group of philanthropic foundations, private corporations, and interested individuals, as well as income on its capital fund. About 35 percent of the Institute's resources in our latest fiscal year were provided by contributors from outside the United States. The GE Foundation provided generous support for this study.

The Executive Committee of the Institute's Board of Directors bears overall responsibility for the Institute's direction, gives general guidance and approval to its research program, and evaluates its performance in pursuit of its mission. The Institute's President is responsible for the identification of topics that are likely to become important over the medium term (one to three years) that should be addressed by Institute scholars. This rolling agenda is set in close consultation with the Institute's research staff and Board of Directors, as well as other stakeholders.

The President makes the final decision to publish any individual Institute study, following independent internal and external review of the work.

The Institute hopes that its research and other activities will contribute to building a stronger foundation for international economic policy around the world. We invite readers of these publications to let us know how they think we can best accomplish this objective.

ADAM S. POSEN, President
August 2013

Authors' Note

The research underlying this study was supported by the GE Foundation. For findings presented in chapters 3 and 4, the statistical analysis of firm-level data on US multinational corporations was conducted at the US Department of Commerce's Bureau of Economic Analysis under arrangements that maintain legal confidentiality requirements. The views expressed are ours and do not reflect official positions of the US Department of Commerce.

GARY CLYDE HUFBAUER
THEODORE H. MORAN
LINDSAY OLDENSKI

Executive Summary

This study examines the relationship between outward foreign direct investment (FDI) by US multinational corporations (MNCs) and US exports, jobs, and research and development (R&D). Using the most appropriate advanced econometric techniques, the study finds that expanded activity at foreign affiliates of US corporations is associated with more production, greater employment, higher exports, and more R&D in the United States. These results are reinforced by a new set of case studies illustrating how overseas and domestic R&D facilities within US MNCs reinforce, complement, and strengthen each other. The findings suggest that less investment abroad by US firms would weaken—not strengthen—the US economy. It is therefore not in the interests of the United States to adopt tax and regulatory policies that discourage global engagement by US multinationals.

The findings reported here by no means imply that there are only winners and no losers from outward investment. Changing patterns of MNC investment, like changing patterns of technology deployment more generally, contribute to job losses and dislocations for some workers and to new opportunities for others. The appropriate response for home-country authorities is to design adjustment and retraining programs to cushion the impact on those adversely affected, not to impede capital flows and engage in a futile effort to preserve jobs in uncompetitive home-country economic activities.

Key facts and findings about US MNCs reported in this study include the following:

1. US MNCs are major contributors to the American economy.
- In 1982, the first year for which annual employment data were collected, US MNCs employed 18.7 million American workers, 25 percent of the total

civilian workforce. In 2010, the latest year for which data are available, US multinationals employed 22 million American workers or about 20 percent of the total civilian workforce.

- The plants of US multinationals are the most productive in the United States in terms of both total factor productivity and labor productivity. They are also the most technology-intensive and pay the highest wages. The plants of US multinationals show labor productivity 16.6 percent higher than large purely domestic firms and 44.6 percent higher than small US firms. Their total factor productivity is 4.2 percent higher than large purely domestic firms and 11.1 percent higher than small domestic firms.

- The jobs at US multinationals pay higher wages than jobs at purely domestic US firms. The average wage paid (including benefits) to US employees of US MNCs was $69,106 in 2010. This is more than 7 percent higher than the average wage paid by all firms in the United States.

- US MNC parents accounted for 29 percent of all US private-sector investment in 2007 and 74 percent of all US private-sector R&D. In 2010, US MNC capital investment in the domestic economy was $430 billion in comparison to $166 billion outside the United States. Thus, for every $1 invested abroad, US MNCs invested $2.60 at home.

2. US MNCs are both large exporters and large purchasers of goods and services in the US domestic market.

- In 2007, the latest year for which data are available, US MNC purchases from American home-country firms amounted to $6 trillion, some 89 percent of all their purchases.

- In the same year, US MNCs exported goods from the United States valued at $559 billion, accounting for nearly half (49 percent) of all US goods exports in 2007. Of these, $215 billion or 38 percent were shipped directly from US plants to sister affiliates abroad.

- Of the approximately $14.4 trillion in global sales by US MNCs in 2010, more than $9.3 trillion (65 percent) originated in the United States.

- MNCs play a large and growing role in the export of services. Services exports from US parents to their foreign affiliates and from US affiliates to their foreign parent companies totaled $166 billion in 2011, or 28 percent of all US private services exports. This represents an increase of 150 percent for within-firm services exports over a 10-year period, accounting for almost one-third of all the growth in US private services exports over the previous decade.

3. There is a complementary relationship between increases in overseas activity by US MNCs and comparable activity in the US home economy.

- Using the most modern econometric techniques, the analysis presented here shows that increases in four variables (employment, sales, capital expenditures, and R&D) in foreign affiliates of US firms are all positively associated with five variables in the United States (employment, sales, capital expenditures, R&D, and exports). All of these positive relationships are significant at the 1 percent level over 20 years of observations across some 1,500 firms.

- Across all fronts, an increase in FDI by a US MNC is associated with an increase in domestic US activities by that same firm. When a US firm increases the employment at its foreign affiliates by 10 percent, employment by that same firm in the United States goes up by an average of 4 percent. Capital expenditures and exports from the United States by that firm also increase by about 4 percent. R&D spending, which is associated not just with overall US employment but also with employment in highly skilled and highly paid jobs, increases by 5.4 percent.

- On the basis of these findings, US policymakers can expect that measures taken to impede or retard US MNC expansion abroad will weaken job creation, investment, R&D, and exports at home, rather than strengthening or enhancing domestic economic activity.

4. These findings on the global activities of US MNCs have important implications for US tax policy.

- Given the high-wage, high-value-added, and R&D-intensive nature of the operations of US MNCs, the United States will want to search for ways to heighten the appeal of the country as a base for the operations of such firms. To accomplish this, the United States badly needs to reform its corporate tax system, both with respect to earnings at home and abroad.

- At 39 percent, the US statutory corporate tax rate (federal and state combined) is the highest among Organization for Economic Cooperation and Development (OECD) countries—11 percentage points higher than the unweighted average of competing countries. The US average effective tax rate is second highest. The US marginal effective corporate tax rate is the highest among OECD and big emerging-market countries.

- To reform the US corporate tax code, the Simpson-Bowles Commission and others have proposed that the federal corporate rate should be cut to 25 percent or lower. This proposal is a sensible start.

- To make the United States more competitive as a location for international business operations, the country should adopt a territorial tax system, as have the great majority of developed countries. This would mean that the active business income of foreign affiliates would be subject to a sharply lower (or zero) rate of taxation in the United States.

1

Overview

Foreign direct investment (FDI) has grown over the past three decades to become a central force in global economic activity. While world nominal GDP has increased fourfold and world bilateral trade flows have grown more than sixfold since 1980, the stock of FDI has swelled by roughly 20 times over from an already reasonably large base. Today the global sales of foreign affiliates of multinational corporations (MNCs) equal roughly two times the amount of total world exports, making foreign investors considerably more important than trade in delivering goods and services around the globe. Within the realm of trade, MNCs are the largest players in arm's-length transactions, and one-third of the movement of goods and services across borders takes place within their intrafirm networks. MNCs account for about half of the world's total research and development (R&D) expenditure and more than two-thirds of the world's business R&D. The bulk of technology flows between countries takes place within the confines of MNC production systems.

The Peterson Institute for International Economics (PIIE) has launched a twin effort to address the implications of this growing role of multinational corporate investment for the US economy. This study on outward FDI from the United States is a sister volume to the 2013 PIIE study on inward FDI into the United States by Theodore H. Moran and Lindsay Oldenski. These two volumes come to a common conclusion: The policy challenge in the years ahead is to create a more favorable setting for multinational investors to locate their best jobs, most beneficial operations, and most dynamic activities here in the United States. As US MNCs expand their global operations, they become more productive, expand output, hire more workers, and conduct more R&D at home and abroad. Thus it is in the interest of the United States to create a policy environment that encourages the growth of both US MNCs investing abroad and foreign MNCs investing in the United States.

While the increasing importance of multinational corporate investment in the international economy represents an opportunity, it also generates understandable apprehension. This study addresses one of the most widespread sources of apprehension—concerns about the consequences for the US home economy as American MNCs spread technology and reposition production around the globe.

The concern about outward investment by US multinationals is certainly not new. The origins go back to the Burke-Hartke legislation (sponsored by the AFL-CIO) in the 1970s and appeared to culminate—at least rhetorically—with Ross Perot's prediction in 1992 that the North American Free Trade Agreement would result in a "giant sucking sound" as jobs migrated south of the border. If today's rhetoric on the issue is slightly less colorful, it is often no less intense, with President Barack Obama earnestly pledging to end tax breaks for corporations that ship jobs overseas.[1]

But what does the evidence show to be the most beneficial US policy toward outward investment by US multinationals? The answer depends on whether outward FDI by these multinational firms—in expanded production and assembly and in the new phenomenon of more R&D conducted abroad—comes at the expense of home-country economic interests or whether, in contrast, this spread of US multinational activities around the globe complements and strengthens the home economy.

Apprehension about outward investment by US multinationals springs from three distinct fears: first, that such investment replaces production of goods and exports of products that might be undertaken at US MNC plants at home; second, that outward investment by US-based MNCs siphons away capital, replacing investment that might be made at home; and third, that the globalization of R&D weakens America's technological capabilities by placing those capabilities elsewhere. The common theme in each of these fears is that outward investment by US-based MNCs is a win-lose phenomenon that harms the American economy.

Each source of apprehension is subject to empirical analysis. For each of the three, it is possible to examine how the home operations of US MNCs have changed as these firms have expanded or contracted their foreign operations. Based on the observed behavior of some 1,500 US MNCs over two decades, we can address the question of whether the US economy would likely be better or worse off if US policies (in particular tax policy) were to be reconfigured to make it harder for US multinationals to carry out operations abroad.

This is the empirical investigation undertaken in this study. First, however, it is important to establish the importance of this issue for American policymakers by examining the role that US MNCs play in the domestic economy and by carefully tracing how their operations within the United States have evolved over time.

---

1. The statement by the president reads: "We don't need a President who plans to ship more jobs overseas, or wants to give more tax breaks to companies that are shipping jobs overseas." "Remarks by the President at a Campaign Event," White House press release, July 16, 2012, www.whitehouse. gov/the-press-office/2012/07/16/remarks-president-campaign-event (accessed on March 25, 2013).

2

Role of US MNCs in the US Economy and Evolution of Their Domestic Operations

A US multinational corporation is defined as a business enterprise headquartered in the United States that has a 10 percent ownership stake or more in at least one affiliate in another country (Barefoot and Mataloni 2009). In absolute numbers, the ranks of US MNCs are rather small, comprising less than 1 percent of all US firms: In 2009 there were 2,347 US MNCs with 26,961 foreign affiliates. But US MNCs continue to have a disproportionately large economic impact on the US home economy—they generate about 20 percent of total US employment and about 25 percent of total US output. It is important to note that their operations remain overwhelmingly concentrated in the home economy. In 2010, the latest year for which data are available, US MNCs generated total value added of $3.9 trillion, with more than 71 percent located in the United States and the remainder abroad. They employed 21.7 million workers in the United States and 10.8 million abroad.

MNC Employment and Output

Over time, US MNCs have increased employment and output in an absolute sense, with their share of total US output and employment fluctuating along with US and global economic factors. In 1982, the first year for which annual employment data were collected, US MNCs employed 18.7 million American workers (25 percent of the total civilian workforce); in 2010, they employed 22 million workers (about 20 percent of the total civilian workforce). In 1994, the first year for which annual output data were collected, the value of domestic output by US MNCs was $1.3 trillion, or 24 percent of total private US output; in 2007, the value of domestic output was $2.6 trillion, or 24 percent of total private US output. In cyclical terms, US MNC output and employment both

Figure 2.1 Year-over-year change in number of employees of US MNCs at home and abroad, 1998–2010

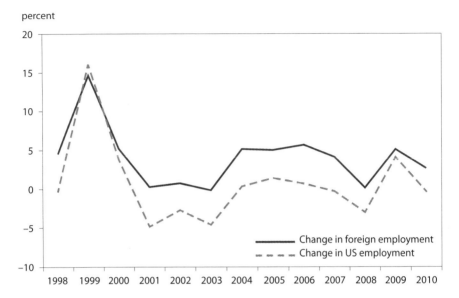

percent

Note: Data are for nonbank US parents and nonbank majority-owned affiliates of US firms. Figures for 2010 are based on preliminary data releases.

Source: Bureau of Economic Analysis, www.bea.gov.

peaked in 2000, then started to decline, with output rebounding in 2003 and employment rebounding over 2004–06.

Between 1984 and 2004, US MNCs expanded employment at their foreign affiliates by 3.8 million and at their home operations by 3.2 million. From 1990 to 2000, this ratio was particularly beneficial for the United States, as US MNCs created almost two jobs at home for each job created abroad. Between 2000 and 2003, however, US MNCs continued to expand employment abroad but decreased the number of jobs at home (during the downturn in the US business cycle after the dot-com bubble burst). Then, between 2004 and 2009, US MNCs returned to expanding payrolls both at home and abroad, adding 1.9 million jobs in the United States and 2.1 million jobs overseas (Barefoot and Mataloni 2009). Figure 2.1 shows these changes year by year.

Under the umbrella of complementary job creation, it is logical to expect that US MNCs will create jobs in line with relative growth rates in the countries where they have operations, with the United States sometimes growing more slowly than other markets. The types of operations conducted by US MNCs in the home country are likely to be more capital-intensive, R&D-intensive, and skill-intensive—and hence fewer in number than more labor-intensive production and assembly activities in the developing world. Maria Borga and Robert

Lipsey (2009) show that US parent firms are more capital-intensive than their foreign affiliates and that affiliates located in developed countries are more capital-intensive than those located in developing countries. An assessment of the strength of the contribution that US MNCs make to the home-country economy should not depend upon a simple comparison of the number of jobs created or the growth rate of job creation by US MNCs at home or abroad. Instead, the focus should be on the determinants of job creation in each location, as well as on whether increasing employment at foreign affiliates facilitates or undermines job creation in the United States. We undertake this exercise in chapter 3 using data on more than 1,500 US MNCs over a 20-year period. However, before moving on to the firm-level analysis, it is useful to start with the aggregate picture.

Figure 2.1 shows the movement of employment at US MNCs in the United States as well as at their foreign affiliates from 1998 through 2010. Some of the dramatic spike that occurs in 1999 reflects improvements in the coverage of US Bureau of Economic Analysis (BEA) surveys of MNCs in 1999. Estimates that adjust for this increase in coverage relative to 1998 suggest that the actual employment change for parents and affiliates was about 0.4 percent (Mataloni and Yorgason 2002). Even with this onetime adjustment, it is clear from the figure that employment by US MNCs at home and abroad moves together. In addition, employment in both locations is highly cyclical. For example, US MNCs increased employment both in the United States and at their foreign affiliates in the late 1990s. However, when the dot-com bubble burst in 2000, they cut employment in all locations. MNC employment in the United States and abroad recovered and began to grow again in the early 2000s. However, the most recent recession led to a fall in US MNC employment worldwide. Employment grew sharply in 2009 and then remained flat (growth rate of 0) in 2010, which is the most recent year for which data are available. This growth in US MNC employment is especially noteworthy when compared with overall US labor demand. According to the US Bureau of Labor Statistics, total private employment in the United States in 2009 fell by 5.3 percent, to 108 million from 114 million in 2008. So both US MNCs and US affiliates of non-US MNCs were adding jobs while the overall private sector in the United States was losing them.

Figure 2.2 shows growth rates for the total sales by US multinationals that originate in the United States, as well as sales by US MNCs originating in their foreign affiliates. Total sales are a good proxy for the amount of production done in a given location. As with employment, sales by US MNCs originating from the United States and from their foreign affiliates generally move together. The exception is 2009, the peak of the recession. In that year, US MNC sales originating at home grew by 2.4 percent relative to the previous year, while sales originating at the foreign affiliates of US firms fell by 8.2 percent. Capital expenditures followed a similar pattern but were slower to rebound from the most recent recession relative to employment and sales, with positive growth in 2010 (figure 2.3). As with figure 2.1, some portion of the spike

Figure 2.2 Year-over-year change in sales of US MNCs at home and abroad, 1998–2010

percent

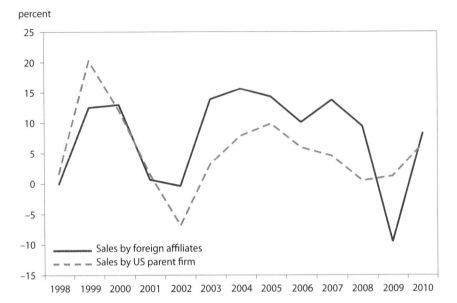

Note: Data are for nonbank US parents and nonbank majority-owned affiliates of US firms. Figures for 2010 are based on preliminary data releases.

Source: Bureau of Economic Analysis, www.bea.gov.

Figure 2.3 Year-over-year change in capital expenditures of US MNCs at home and abroad, 1998–2010

percent

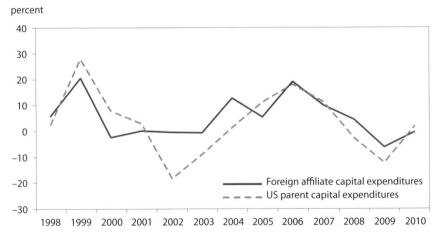

Note: Data are for nonbank US parents and nonbank majority-owned affiliates of US firms. Figures for 2010 are based on preliminary data releases.

Source: Bureau of Economic Analysis, www.bea.gov.

in sales and capital expenditures for 1999 reflects methodological changes to the BEA surveys that took place that year. But the overall trends and values for other years are not affected by these changes.

To get a sense of the magnitudes being discussed here, US MNCs employed 21.6 million people in the United States and 10.8 million in other countries in 2010. Of the approximately $14.4 trillion in global sales by US MNCs in that year, more than $9.3 trillion worth originated in the United States and the rest in foreign affiliates.

The principal contribution that US MNCs can make to the US home economy is to reallocate economic activity in ways that raise US living standards. Benefits emerge not only in the form of new, better, cheaper, and more reliable goods and services that US MNCs produce at home and import from abroad but also from the competition they generate in the economy more broadly. Popular discussion often focuses on US MNC job creation at home—especially "good" jobs with high wages and good benefits. One potential drawback associated with the expansion of "good" jobs in the United States is that while an increase in the demand for more highly skilled workers relative to less-skilled workers will increase average wages, it can also widen the wage gap between workers at the top and the bottom of the income distribution. This possibility will be revisited in more detail in chapter 3.

Empirical studies consistently show that more imports and exports create significant payoffs in terms of higher GDP. To cite one study, Gary Hufbauer, Jeffrey J. Schott, and Woan Foong Wong (2010, box 1.2) estimated both trade gains and associated GDP gains that might have been generated by a highly successful outcome of the World Trade Organization's Doha Round. Based on a sample of 22 countries, the authors concluded that each additional $1 billion of two-way trade would deliver GDP gains of about $400 million—a high payoff indeed.[1] The fact that MNCs export and import more than purely domestic firms implies that MNCs provide greater GDP gains to the home economy.

Another key measurement is the specific kinds of jobs and activities that US MNCs generate at home. It is important to note that the plants of US MNCs are the most productive plants in the United States in terms of both total factor productivity and labor productivity. They are also the most technology-intensive and pay the highest wages. US MNC parents accounted for 29 percent of all US private-sector investment in 2007 and 74 percent of all US private-sector R&D. The plants of US MNCs show labor productivity 16.6 percent higher than that of large domestic firms and 44.6 percent higher than that of small firms.[2] Their total factor productivity is 4.2 percent higher than that of large domestic firms and 11.1 percent higher than that of small

---

1. The payoff results from higher productivity, greater variety, sifting and sorting of firms, and old-fashioned comparative advantage. The results cited do not reflect simple multiplier analysis, as the trade gains in question are balanced (additional imports approximately equal additional exports).

2. See Doms and Jensen (1998) and Bernard, Jensen, and Schott (2009).

Table 2.1 Operations of firms located in the United States, 2009

	All US firms	US multinational corporations
Annual wage per worker (dollars)	64,552	69,208
Imports/exports ratio	1.24	1.21
R&D/sales ratio	0.018	0.021

Sources: Bureau of Economic Analysis, www.bea.gov; US Census Bureau, www.census.gov.

domestic firms. The plants of US multinationals use more technologies from the *Survey of Manufacturing Technology* list of 17 advanced manufacturing technologies than do large or small domestic firms. Finally, the jobs at US multinationals pay higher wages than do purely domestic US firms. Table 2.1 shows that the average wage paid (including benefits) to US employees of US MNCs was $69,208 in 2009. This is more than 7 percent higher than the average wage paid by all firms in the United States.

In addition to the high productivity, high value added, and high wages of US MNC parents in the United States, US MNCs purchase large amounts of goods and services from domestic suppliers and account for a sizable amount of US exports. In 2007, US MNC purchases from American home-country firms amounted to $6 trillion, some 89 percent of all their purchases. In the same year, US MNCs exported goods from the United States valued at $559 billion, nearly half (49 percent) of all US goods exports. Of these, $215 billion or 38 percent were shipped directly from US plants to sister affiliates abroad. US MNCs also export relatively more and import relatively less compared with purely domestic firms, and they invest more in R&D (table 2.1). They also play a large and growing role in the export of services. Services exports from US parents to their foreign affiliates and from US affiliates to their foreign parent companies totaled $166 billion in 2011, or 28 percent of all US private services exports (accounting for almost one-third of all the growth in US private services exports) over the previous decade. Underscoring the MNC role as a vehicle for services exports, figure 2.4 shows that while exports of services that took place outside MNC networks fell by 7 percent at the trough of the recession in 2009, exports of services by MNCs never experienced negative growth and rebounded to grow by 10 percent from 2010 to 2011. The United States shows a strong comparative advantage in exports of high-wage, high-skill services, and US MNCs and US affiliates of foreign MNCs are likely to remain an important channel for exploiting this comparative advantage (Jensen 2011).

Industry-Level Patterns in Activities of US MNCs

Figures 2.1, 2.2, and 2.3 shed light on important aggregate trends in MNC investment. However, underlying these overall patterns are actions of many

Figure 2.4 Year-over-year change in services exports within and outside MNCs, 2000–2011

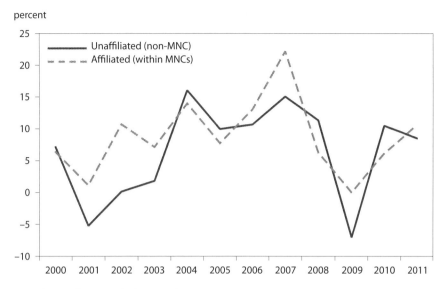

percent

Source: Bureau of Economic Analysis, www.bea.gov.

very different firms operating in different industries. For example, the aggregate trends cannot tell us whether growth in foreign activity is happening across the board at all US firms or whether a small number of large players in certain industries are driving the overall trends.

A first step in disaggregating the difference is to break the trends down by industry. Figure 2.5 shows the growth in employment at foreign affiliates of manufacturing firms, broken down by subsectors within manufacturing. Figure 2.6 shows the same information for nonmanufacturing industries. The highest growth has been in retail, management, professional services, and accommodation and food services. Retail and accommodation and food services are industries where exporting is extremely difficult if not impossible. This suggests that much of the US MNC expansion abroad in these industries has sought out new markets to sell goods and services and not as a substitute for US production workers. When Wal-Mart, Hilton, or McDonalds opens a new branch in a foreign country, they are not doing so at the expense of US workers. Instead, they are expanding to serve an entirely new customer base. Management and professional services can be exported as stand-alone services, but they are still sold through foreign direct investment (FDI) abroad in much larger volumes than through exports (Oldenski 2012). Hence, outward FDI in these sectors largely generates sales to new foreign customers rather than shifting activities abroad that otherwise would have been performed in the United States.

Figure 2.5   Employment at foreign affiliates of US MNCs, manufacturing industries, 1999–2009

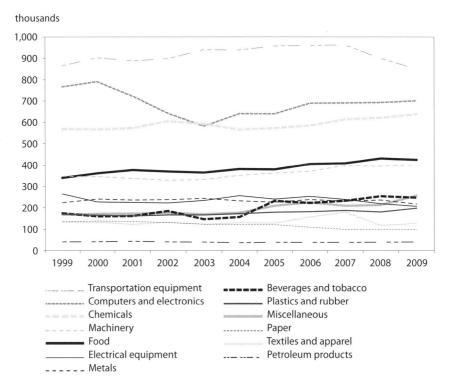

thousands

Transportation equipment ∙∙∙∙∙ ∙∙∙ ∙∙∙∙∙
Computers and electronics ∙∙∙∙∙∙∙∙∙∙∙∙∙
Chemicals
Machinery ∙∙ ∙∙∙ ∙∙ ∙∙∙
Food
Electrical equipment
Metals ∙ ∙ ∙ ∙ ∙ ∙

Beverages and tobacco ■■ ■■ ■■
Plastics and rubber
Miscellaneous
Paper ∙∙∙∙∙∙∙∙∙∙∙
Textiles and apparel
Petroleum products ∙∙∙ ∙∙∙ ∙

Note: Data for 2009 are based on preliminary releases.

Source: Bureau of Economic Analysis, www.bea.gov.

A similar phenomenon may also apply to manufacturing firms, though not to the same extent. For example, table 2.2 shows that in 2009 only 9 percent of all sales by foreign affiliates of US MNCs were to the United States. The majority of sales went to the country in which the affiliate was located (61 percent) or to other countries (30 percent). For manufacturing firms, the numbers were not that different, with only 11 percent of foreign affiliate sales going to the United States and 55 percent to the local market.

Figure 2.6   Employment at foreign affiliates of US MNCs, nonmanufacturing industries, 1999–2009

thousands

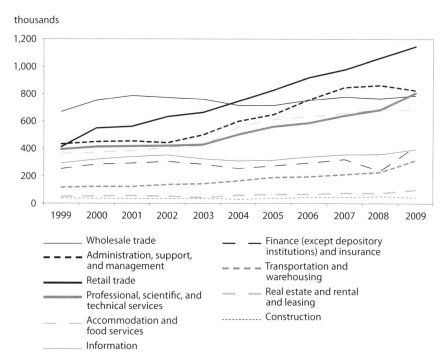

Wholesale trade

– – – – Administration, support, and management

Retail trade

Professional, scientific, and technical services

Accommodation and food services

Information

— — Finance (except depository institutions) and insurance

═ ═ ═ Transportation and warehousing

Real estate and rental and leasing

············ Construction

Note: Data for 2009 are based on preliminary releases.

Source: Bureau of Economic Analysis, www.bea.gov.

Table 2.2   Foreign affiliate sales by destination, 2009

	Total sales	Sales to the United States	Sales to the local market	Sales to other countries
All industries				
Value (millions of dollars)	4,857,010	432,005	2,953,315	1,471,690
Share (percent)	100	9	61	30
Manufacturing				
Value (millions of dollars)	2,039,525	225,047	1,124,903	689,575
Share (percent)	100	11	55	34

Note: Figures are based on preliminary data releases.

Source: Bureau of Economic Analysis, www.bea.gov.

3

Outward FDI by US MNCs: Implications for US Jobs, Exports, and Investment

The previous chapter showed the role that US multinational corporations play in the US domestic economy. Does evidence from the United States indicate that outward investment by US MNCs substitutes for production at home and for exports that otherwise could be made from the home economy? Does outward investment destroy jobs that otherwise would remain competitive in the United States? Or does outward investment by US MNCs actually expand production and exports within the US domestic economy in comparison to what the outcome would be if these MNCs were not able to expand abroad so readily? Likewise, does investment in other countries by US MNCs substitute for investment in the US home market?

Finding answers to these questions may appear straightforward at first glance. It is not difficult to document that MNCs invest more at home and export more from home plants than do typical or average home-country firms.

The McKinsey Global Institute (2010), for example, reports that US multinationals make a disproportionate contribution to the US economy in comparison to other firms along a number of metrics. So does Matthew J. Slaughter (2010), and both McKinsey and Slaughter examine the same Bureau of Economic Analysis (BEA) data as does this study.

But however convincing those data may be, these are not necessarily fair tests because MNCs are not "typical" or "average"—they are larger and more capital- and technology-intensive, engage in more advertising, and have other characteristics that set them apart from purely domestic firms. US MNCs should therefore be expected to perform better than other companies. This methodological insight continues to be neglected in popular debate. Perhaps MNCs should be expected to invest even more at home and produce and export from home plants.

Outward Investment, Production at Home, and Exports: What the Record Shows

Early work on the substitution hypothesis came with the publication of *American Multinationals and American Interests* in 1978 by C. Fred Bergsten, Thomas Horst, and Theodore H. Moran, with Horst (chapter 3) being the analytic pioneer in this endeavor. To discover whether US MNCs substitute production abroad for exports from the US home economy, Horst argued that what is needed is to compare "likes with likes." For example, one needs to compare the export behavior of large firms that undertake outward investment with the export behavior of large firms that do not undertake outward investment; compare the export behavior of smaller firms that undertake outward investment with the export behavior of smaller firms that do not undertake outward investment; compare the export behavior of firms with high R&D or extensive advertising that undertake outward investment with the export behavior of firms with high R&D or extensive advertising that do not undertake outward investment; and so forth. While this methodology was not able to capture the true "counterfactual scenario"—namely, what a given MNC would have done had it not had the option of using foreign direct investment (FDI)—the analysis was at least able to control for some key characteristics of firms such as size and R&D intensity.

This set of like-with-like comparisons showed that US firms that undertake outward investment actually achieve higher levels of exports as a percentage of domestic shipments than do firms that stay at home in the United States. Further, this superior export performance—which demonstrates superior competitiveness in the face of global pressures—is larger for firms with more extensive global operations. The percentage of domestic shipments that leaves the home market destined for external markets is larger for MNCs that engage in larger amounts of international investment. This demonstrates the key point that outward investment by US MNCs enhances the competitiveness of their home-country operations, measured in comparison to similar kinds of firms that do not undertake outward investment or that do not undertake as much outward investment. By this measure, outward investment appears to be a complement to greater production at home, not a substitute for it.

A literature review of subsequent studies using more advanced statistical techniques shows repeated findings of complementarity between MNC outward investment and exports from a more competitive industrial base at home. An early study by Robert Lipsey and Merle Yahr Weiss (1981) found a positive correlation (after controlling for firm characteristics) between outward investment and exports for all levels of investment. Moreover, the authors discovered that the level of manufacturing activity in a given country by US firms was positively associated with US exports from the same industries to that country and negatively associated with exports by producers of rival nationalities. Along the same lines, they noted that the presence of affiliates of non-US MNCs in a given country was negatively related to US exports to that country and positively related to exports for the home countries of the non-US MNCs. In a somewhat mercantile vein, they concluded that direct investment by US MNCs in any one country tended to increase US exports and market shares in that country and reduce those of producers of rival nationalities and that the operations of non-US MNCs tended to raise home-country exports and market shares and reduce those of US firms. Thus, a smaller US MNC presence abroad would reduce MNC exports and the US market share in other countries. Their counterfactual outcome was the same as the scenario portrayed by Horst: Making home-country MNCs cut back on outward investment hurts the access of home-country workers to export-related jobs.

Next in line in the literature review is a study again by Lipsey and Yahr Weiss (1984) that showed that the complementarity between outward investment and domestic exports was strong not only for intermediate goods sent abroad for further processing but also for the exports of finished products shipped by parent US firms. This study also found that a higher proportion of foreign operations by US firms was associated with higher average compensation at home. Mary Amiti and Katharine Wakelin (2002) also found evidence of complementarities between exports and FDI.

It is important to note that complementarity is not an idiosyncratic finding about outward investment by US MNCs. When Swedish MNCs were subjected to criticism from domestic labor, Magnus Blomström, Robert Lipsey, and Ksenia Kulchyck (1988) undertook a study that found a similar complementary relationship between outward investment by Swedish multinationals and home-country exports and employment. Outward investment by Japanese MNCs shows the same kinds of effects at home (Lipsey, Ramstetter, and Blomström 2000). The complementarity is almost as great for manufacturing as for distribution. Keith Head and John Ries (2001) calculate that a 10 percent increase in FDI abroad in manufacturing and distribution would increase exports from home plants in Japan by 1.2 and 1.5 percent, respectively.

To summarize, the demonstration of complementarity has been a regular feature of empirical investigation (Markusen and Maskus 2003). When labor substitution does show up in the data, it is almost entirely limited to competition between alternative low-wage locations in the developing world rather than vertically between parent and affiliates in lesser-developed regions (Brainard and Riker 1997).

Further evidence about whether outward investment might be transferring production abroad that otherwise would remain competitive at home can be found by comparing unit values of production at home with overseas plants in the developing world. If outward investment by multinationals were simply relocating production from the home economy to developing countries, one would expect, as argued by Lawrence Edwards and Robert Lawrence (2013), a rise in unit values for production and exports of goods by affiliates in developing countries. But the authors find within-sector unit values to be much lower in the new developing-country plants than in the home market—for example, between 15 and 30 percent of medium- and high-technology products exported by the United States in comparison with affiliates in China—and they find no change in these relative unit values over the entire 16-year period from 1990 to 2006. They conclude that what is taking place is production-fragmentation through outward FDI—in other words, the transfer of low-skill-intensive and low-unit-value operations abroad, rather than the production relocation of higher-skill-intensive and higher-unit-value operations in which the United States continues to enjoy a comparative advantage.

Outward Investment and Investment at Home: What the Record Shows

Turning to the contention that outward investment by US MNCs "drains off" capital that otherwise would be invested at home, the evidence also suggests complementarities rather than zero-sum dynamics in parent MNC strategy. Mihir Desai, C. Fritz Foley, and James R. Hines (2005) found that years in which US MNCs make greater capital expenditures abroad coincide with greater capital spending by the same firms at home.

Of course, the correlation between the domestic and foreign growth rates of MNCs might occur for other reasons than an interaction between operations in both locales. For example, a pharmaceutical company may discover a new drug or a software company may develop a new process that leads to simultaneous increases in activity at home and abroad. So Desai, Foley, and Hines (2009) use an instrumental variable that predicts foreign investment but does not directly reflect domestic operations. Their instrumental variable is a firm-specific weighted average of foreign GDP growth, which can be used to forecast growth rates of foreign investment in that country by the MNC. These predicted growth rates in turn can be traced back to explain possibly related changes in home-country activity by the MNC. Using this procedure, they find that 10 percent greater foreign investment by the MNC triggers 2.2 percent additional domestic investment. They show that there are similar positive relationships between foreign investment and home-country exports, R&D spending, numbers of employees, and employee compensation.

Finally, looking specifically at one of the most sensitive target locations for outward investment—China—Lee Branstetter and C. Fritz Foley (2010) find that US firms that invest in China simultaneously invest more in the US home market as well.

New Empirical Evidence: The Complementary Relationship between Domestic and Foreign Expansion by US MNCs

This section offers new evidence using sophisticated analytical techniques to investigate the relationship between MNC expansion at home and abroad. When firms increase their foreign activity, is it at the expense of US employment? Or is it part of a larger expansion strategy that allows for greater production and employment at home as well as abroad? Do increases in foreign affiliate activity lead to productivity gains that increase employment, wages, production, and investment in the United States as well as abroad? In other words, taking a fresh look at an old question, do the activities of US MNCs at home and abroad complement or substitute for one another?

To disentangle the extent to which MNC activity at home and abroad are substitutes or complements, we have examined a trove of detailed information on how individual firms behave over time. The BEA collects confidential firm-level data on the activities of US-owned multinationals, both at home and at their foreign affiliates. All US-owned firms with at least one foreign affiliate that meet a minimum size threshold are required by law to provide these data to the BEA. These comprehensive firm-level data allow us to examine what happens when an individual firm expands its FDI activities.

For this exercise, we employ panel regression methods that use data on all US MNCs over a 20-year period. We include firm "fixed effects," which allow us to examine changes within each firm over time, rather than comparing one firm with another. Firm fixed effects hold constant everything that is unique about a given firm, isolating how its employment in the United States and the other variables we examine change when the firm increases its outward FDI. Thus, all the characteristics that define a given firm—such as the industry it operates in, its size, and its relative market power—are controlled for and do not confound the results. This is a significant advance over the early Bergsten, Horst, and Moran (1978) approach, which was limited to comparing US firms that invested abroad with other US firms that did not invest abroad (or did less investing abroad). We also include year fixed effects, a technique that gets rid of any potential impact of recessions and booms. Just as firm fixed effects hold firm characteristics constant, year fixed effects hold constant everything external to the firm that was going on in a given year. The only way to truly identify a causal effect between foreign and domestic activity would be to randomly assign some firms to become multinationals, while forcing others to remain purely domestic. This type of pure experiment is neither possible nor desirable. However, using the fixed-effects methodology is the next best option, as this approach controls for everything that is unique about a given firm and looks at changes within each firm over time, rather than drawing conclusions based on observed behaviors across very different firms.

Figure 3.1 summarizes the relationship between US MNC activities at home and abroad. These results draw on firm-level data from 1990 through 2009, covering more than 1,500 US MNCs and their more than 10,000 affiliates. The analysis controls for trends over time, thus isolating the relationship between FDI and domestic activities separate from the effects of aggregate growth rates and business cycles. It also controls for the identity of the firm, thus removing any concerns about firm-specific drivers of these trends, such as how big the firm is or what type of goods or services it produces.[1] The first thing to note about the relationships between FDI and domestic growth

---

1. For more details on the statistical results, see table A.1 in appendix A.

Figure 3.1 Increases in foreign activity of US MNCs are accompanied by increases in domestic activity

a. A 10 percent increase in employment at foreign affiliates leads to:

percent

R&D spending in the US	+5.4
Capital expenditures in the US	+4.3
Exports from the US	+4.2
US sales	+4.1
US employment	+3.9

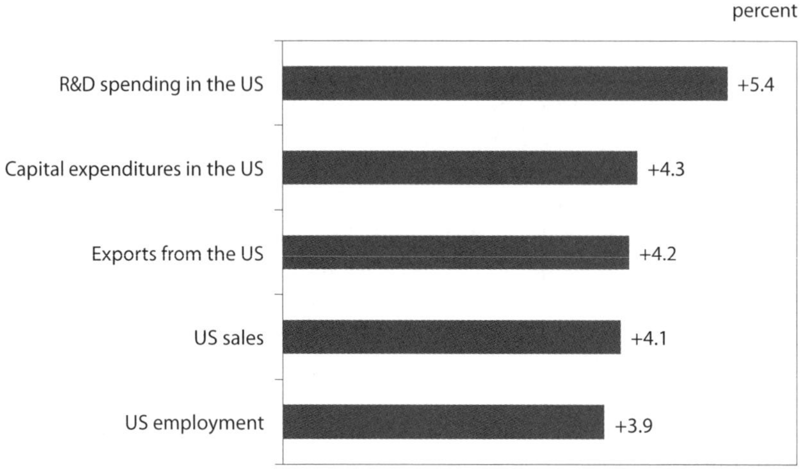

b. A 10 percent increase in sales by foreign affiliates leads to:

percent

R&D spending in the US	+7.0
Capital expenditures in the US	+2.5
Exports from the US	+3.3
US sales	+2.6
US employment	+2.3

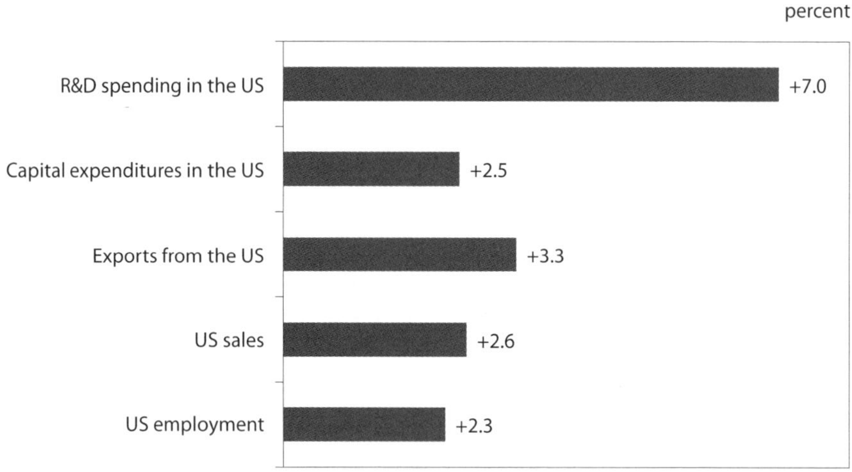

(continues on next page)

presented in figure 3.1 is that they are all positive. By any measure, increasing FDI by a US firm is associated with an increase in domestic US activities by that same firm. When a US firm increases the employment at its foreign affiliates by 10 percent, employment by that same firm in the United States goes up by an average of 4 percent. Capital expenditures and exports from the United

Figure 3.1 Increases in foreign activity of US MNCs are accompanied by increases in domestic activity *(continued)*

c. A 10 percent increase in R&D at foreign affiliates leads to:

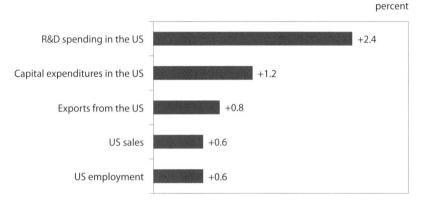

d. A 10 percent increase in capital expenditures at foreign affiliates leads to:

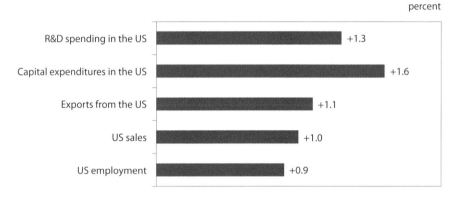

Note: All results are statistically significant at the 1 percent level. See appendix A for a more detailed regression table.

Source: Based on regressions using firm-level data for 1990–2009 from the Bureau of Economic Analysis, www.bea.gov.

States by that firm also increase by about 4 percent. R&D spending, which is associated not just with overall US employment but with employment in highly skilled and highly paid jobs, increases by 5.4 percent.[2] The results are similar when increases in FDI are measured by affiliate sales or capital expenditures instead of employment.

---

2. The case studies of globalization of R&D in chapter 4 illustrate how this might occur.

Projecting differential growth rates between the United States and emerging-market economies two decades into the future raises the possibility that by 2030, US MNCs might employ more workers abroad and invest more abroad than in the United States. But we do not view this prospect as cause for alarm so long as MNC expansion abroad complements expansion at home—which indeed has been the experience of the past two decades.

It is useful to dwell for a moment on precisely what conclusions can and cannot be drawn from this analysis. With regard to causation, it is not possible to claim with certainty that the expansion of foreign affiliate activity causes some specific reaction in domestic activity. As noted above, the only way to definitively identify a causal effect between foreign and domestic activity would be to randomly assign some firms to become multinationals, while forcing others to remain purely domestic, which is an implausible pure experiment. A more practical approach is to observe what happens to the domestic operations of US MNCs when they expand abroad, but to do so in a way that controls for other characteristics of the firms in question, as well as for the overall global economy at the time of the expansion. Here our econometric analysis shows that increases in four variables (employment, sales, capital expenditures, and R&D) in foreign affiliates of US firms are all positively associated with five variables in the United States (employment, sales, exports, capital expenditures, and R&D spending), with all of these positive relationships significant at the 1 percent confidence level over 20 years of observations.

What about a counterfactual scenario? What would happen at home if MNC expansion abroad were limited or made more difficult? It is impossible to know precisely what would happen at home if a US firm is engaged in less activity abroad. On the basis of our findings of positive interactions between increases in measures of firm activity at home and firm activity abroad, it is plausible to hypothesize that increasing foreign affiliate activity increases the overall productivity of an MNC in a way that leads to higher employment in all locations, both at home and abroad. If this is the case, then inhibiting overseas expansion would have negative consequences for the US economy. Or, it could happen that US exports and greater US employment follow foreign affiliate activity, for example, by providing postsales services or parts and maintenance. Again, if this is the case, then inhibiting overseas expansion would have negative consequences for the US economy.

Our findings do not mean that certain aspects of overseas expansion never diminish similar aspects of home-country MNC activity. Quite the contrary, the spread of investment and R&D, like trade in general, is likely to result in reshuffling economic activity within, as well as across, sectors on both sides of borders. In particular, as we discuss later, some studies indicate that the conduct of low-skilled operations in low-wage countries abroad will reduce low-skilled employment in the United States. This is in line with America's comparative advantage in high-skill rather than low-skill production of goods and services. The point is that, given the multiple positive and significant relationships between increases in overseas activity and increases in jobs, sales, exports, capital expenditures, and R&D at home, summarized in figure 3.1, the dispassionate public policy analyst would have to bet that the aggregate result from outward FDI by US firms is strongly positive. Conversely, if overseas operations of US MNCs were restricted or made more difficult, the overall consequences would be less activity at home, not more.

The globalization of R&D by US MNCs has been a source of concern above and beyond overall multinational expansion. Because R&D is a high-skilled activity, its global expansion has been viewed by some as a sign that foreign investment by US MNCs is moving away from just low-skilled assembly work into areas where US workers have traditionally enjoyed a comparative advantage. Yet the expansion of R&D at foreign affiliates is also associated with positive employment and production outcomes for US workers. This topic will be addressed in more detail in the next chapter.

Returning to our main question, however, across all variables examined in figure 3.1, the evidence consistently shows that foreign-affiliate and US activity within a firm move together as complements rather than substitutes. These results should not surprise anyone who is familiar with how firms work. US MNCs are not constrained by a lack of capital or other resources. Rather, their growth is limited by the array of opportunities for profitable investment. When new opportunities arise, whether at home or abroad, the whole enterprise can grow.

How Do the New Results Compare with Other Studies of MNC Investment?

The results presented above differ from previous studies of MNC expansion in several key ways. First, it is absolutely crucial to keep in mind that MNC activity, like all economic activity, is cyclical. One cannot simply choose two years, show the difference in MNC employment between the arbitrary starting and ending points, and call it a trend. Figures 2.1 and 2.2 in chapter 2 illustrated this point. For example, if one were to compare employment by US MNCs at the peak of the technology boom in 2000 with employment at the worst part of the most recent recession in 2008, it would look like these firms were abandoning America by shedding more than 2 million jobs over the early 2000s. This message of doom and gloom is much different than the story one could tell by comparing US MNC employment in 2002 after the dot-com bubble burst with employment in 2009 after the United States began to recover from its most recent trough. Choosing these comparison years would show that US MNCs have added more than 2 million jobs over the selected time period. While 2009 is the most recent year for which US MNC employment data are available, it seems likely that as the overall economic recovery continues, MNC employment in the United States will grow as well.

This study takes several different approaches to dealing with the cyclical nature of economic activity. First, all tables and figures of aggregate trends show information on all years for which data are available, rather than focusing on one point in time or comparing two arbitrary years. Second, the econometric analysis controls directly for trends over time, thus isolating the relationship between MNC activities at home and abroad, separate from the effects of aggregate growth rates and business cycles.

Another consideration is whether or not to include banks in the set of multinationals. This study excludes them and focuses only on nonbank multinationals for two reasons. First, the recent financial crisis affected banking in ways that were not representative of overall multinational activity. Second, the BEA has changed the treatment of banks in its data, which complicates the study of trends over time when banks are included.

Previous studies have focused on manufacturing FDI. However, services are becoming an increasingly important share of multinational activity. Omitting this area of growth has been a weakness of earlier analyses, so both manufacturing and services firms are included in this study. As was shown in figure 2.4 in chapter 2, services exports by US MNCs have been growing rapidly over the past decade. Available evidence suggests that the United States has a comparative advantage in the production and export of high-skilled services and that the globalization of services is likely to be a major source of net-positive economic expansion for the US economy (Jensen 2011).

Perhaps the most innovative feature of this study is to use the latest firm-level data to estimate complementarities between MNC expansion abroad and activities at home. Almost all of the studies on the relationship between foreign and domestic expansion of MNCs described in this chapter were based on country-level or industry-level data.

However, a few prior studies did use firm-level data to examine the relationship between MNC behavior at home and abroad. From a methodological standpoint, the paper most similar to our study was Desai, Foley, and Hines (2009). They use firm-level data from 1982 to 2004 to show that growth in employment, compensation, fixed assets, and property, plant, and equipment at foreign affiliates of US firms is associated with growth at home in these same measures. Our study updates their data with information through 2009 and includes all US MNCs, not just those operating in the manufacturing sector. It also goes beyond the scope of their analysis by looking at the relationship between R&D expansion at foreign affiliates and a number of measures of domestic activity. The results of the two studies, however, tell a similar story: that the foreign and domestic activities of US MNCs are complements, not substitutes.

Harald Oberhofer and Michael Pfaffermayr (2012) use data on about 70,000 European firms to examine the extent to which these firms use exports and FDI as substitutes or complements. They find that while a small number of the firms employ substitution strategies, the majority use FDI and exports as complements.

Although these firm-level studies show that FDI and domestic activities are complements for the average firm, there is also evidence that shows differing degrees and mixes of complementarities and substitution depending on the nature of the FDI. Ann Harrison and Margaret McMillan (2011), using data for manufacturing MNCs through 1999, estimate demand for US labor by US MNCs as a function of wages and the cost of capital in the countries where they have affiliates. This is a different exercise than the one we have carried out. Harrison and McMillan are essentially asking whether firms with affiliates in lower-wage countries employ fewer workers in the United States. They find that lower wages in developing countries are associated with less domestic employment at US manufacturing MNCs but that wages in developed countries have no relationship with US employment. However, these results are small in magnitude, suggesting that having affiliates in developing countries with a 10 percent lower average wage is associated with 0.6 to 1 percent less employment by those US MNCs in the United States (or, conversely, that a 10 percent higher average foreign affiliate wage is associated with 0.6 to 1 percent more US home employment). This says that when MNCs open affiliates in lower-wage countries, they tend to hire fewer workers in the United States, but when they open affiliates in higher-wage countries, they tend to hire more US workers.

However, wages could be picking up something other than labor costs, such as the industry in which the firm is operating. All else being equal, paying lower wages is an indication that the demand for a certain type of worker is relatively low compared with the supply of those workers. Thus, if a given firm is paying lower wages at its foreign affiliates and hiring fewer workers in the United States relative to other firms, it could be that the firm is operating in an industry that would be shrinking in the United States for reasons unrelated to outward investment. Thus, the Harrison and McMillan results do not exclude alternative explanations for the association between outward FDI in the manufacturing sector of low-wage countries and the relative decline in unskilled jobs in the United States.

In a similar study, Helen Simpson (2012) uses data on UK firms and, like Harrison and McMillan, finds that the extent to which domestic employment and outward FDI are complements or substitutes depends on whether the FDI is placed in high-wage or low-wage countries. Firms that invest in low-wage countries are more likely to use FDI as a substitute for exports, but firms that invest in high-wage countries use FDI and exports as complements. This is not surprising, as it reflects patterns of comparative advantage that we would expect to see with trade as well as with FDI. Moreover, for both the United States and the United Kingdom, the overall net effect for the economy is complementarity, as FDI placed in other developed countries (a source of complementarities) is much greater than FDI placed in low-wage countries. As Simpson points out, only 87 UK MNCs in her data invested solely in low-wage countries in 2004, contrasted with 1,941 UK MNCs that invested solely in high-wage countries. In the case of the United States, the top 10 destination countries for FDI by US MNCs are all high-wage countries. Thus, while differences in the mix of substitution and complementarity across firms and FDI destinations have been documented, they do not undermine the net result that, on average, MNCs simultaneously increase employment and other FDI measures at home and abroad, rather than reducing one in favor of the other.

The evidence paints a picture in which outward investment is an integral part of the strategy of MNCs to maximize the competitive position of the whole corporation, a goal for which headquarters raise the needed amount of capital from sources around the globe. In determining where to deploy capital and where to locate production, relative costs—including not only relative wages and benefits but also relative skills and productivity—play a definite role. But in the end, operations at home and operations abroad complement each other as the MNC parent tries to make the deployment of its tangible and intangible assets most productive and therefore most profitable. As pointed out earlier, US MNC plants accounted for 55 percent of all US goods exports in 2009, and 36 percent of those US MNC goods exports were shipped directly to overseas affiliates of the US parent (Barefoot and Mataloni 2011). US MNC capital investment in the domestic economy in 2009 was $410 billion, compared with $186 billion outside the United States. Thus, for every $1 invested abroad, US MNCs invested $2.20 at home. As mentioned earlier, the time may come when US MNCs invest more abroad than they invest in the United States, but so long as a complementary relationship characterizes investment abroad and investment at home, we do not see greater investment abroad as a cause for alarm.

The finding that home-country firms that engage in outward FDI export more from their home plants than similar firms that do not engage in outward investment bears directly on the composition of good jobs/bad jobs in the home-country market. Export-related jobs across all developed countries offer a wage-and-benefit premium in comparison to other jobs in comparable firms. In the United States, export jobs pay wages 10 to 11 percent higher than nonexport-related jobs (Richardson 2005a). Thus, outward investment by US MNCs results in a higher proportion of good jobs (relatively high wages and benefits) compared with bad jobs (relatively low wages and benefits) at home.

One side effect of creating relatively high-paying or "good" jobs in the United States is that the expansion of these jobs increases the demand for more highly skilled workers relative to workers in lower-paid and lower-skilled occupations, which can lead to an increase in income inequality. This tension is not new. The Heckscher-Ohlin and Ricardo-Viner models of international trade have long shown that while a country as a whole will gain in the aggregate from specializing and trading according to comparative advantage, this specialization has distributional effects within the country. Because the United States enjoys a comparative advantage in high-skill, high-wage activities, increased specialization across countries will lead to more of these activities being performed in the United States. However, the United States does not have a comparative advantage in low-skilled, labor-intensive production, which can be more efficiently done in other countries. Thus, increased specialization across countries will have an aggregate positive effect, but these benefits will accrue primarily to more highly skilled workers.

Robert Feenstra and Gordon Hanson (1999) look at the relationship between income inequality within the United States and increases in the vertical fragmentation of production across countries. They show that the gap between high-skilled and low-skilled workers has been growing over the last several decades and that international trade in intermediate goods has been among the contributing factors to this growing divide, as US producers specialize more and more in the high-skill stages of production while offshoring lower-skill tasks.

More recently, David Autor, David Dorn, and Gordon Hanson (2012) have shown that increased manufacturing imports from China negatively affect the wages of US manufacturing workers who compete directly with these imports. Avraham Ebenstein et al. (2009) look at import competition from, and MNC offshoring to, both high- and low-wage countries. They find that offshoring to low-wage countries is associated with wage declines for competing workers, whereas offshoring to high-wage countries is associated with wage increases in the United States.

Evidence that specific groups have been negatively affected by increased global competition does not contradict our findings that, in the aggregate, increased production abroad by US MNCs improves wages and other outcomes in the United States. The findings reported in table 2.1 in chapter 2 by no means imply that there are only winners and no losers from outward investment. Changing patterns of MNC investment—like changing patterns of technology deployment more generally—contribute to job losses and dislocations for some workers as well as to new opportunities for others. The appropriate response for home-country authorities is to design adjustment and retraining programs to cushion the impact on those adversely affected, not to impede capital flows and engage in a futile effort to preserve jobs in uncompetitive home-country economic activities.

The benefits that accrue to US companies that engage in outward investment are not limited to their superior export performance. US MNCs that invest abroad use frontier production processes in their home-country plants more frequently, have higher levels of worker productivity, and enjoy more rapid growth rates of overall productivity than other firms (Bernard, Jensen, and Schott 2009). Taken altogether, as J. David Richardson (2005a) found, American-owned firms that engage in outward investment pay their blue-collar production workers 7 to 15 percent more than comparable nonoutward investors (7 percent more in large US MNC plants, 15 percent more in small US MNC plants). Given their higher productivity and geographic diversification, US firms that invest abroad enjoy lower levels of bankruptcy and are less likely to suffer job loss than similar firms that do not engage in outward investment. This outcome makes intuitive sense but contrasts strongly with conventional wisdom. In other words, contrary to popular perception, outward investment by US MNCs creates a more stable job base at home.

Findings about US multinationals echo what has been discovered elsewhere. EU multinationals that establish affiliates abroad are larger, more profitable, and more productive than firms that do not. Using large firm–level data from 12 countries in the euro area for 2003 and 2006, Ingo Geishecker, Holger Gorg, and Daria Taglioni (2009) report that EU firms that engage in outward investment enjoy a higher rate of productivity growth and a higher survival rate. Better performance is associated with a larger number of affiliates and more locations.

To be sure, these findings do not imply that the home-country industrial sector where the outward investment originates is always expanding on a net basis. What is striking, however, is that US firms that engage in outward investment offer better prospects for their workers than firms that do not, and this holds in both expanding and contracting industries. To use Richardson's (2005a) characterization, home-country companies in contracting sectors that are "globally engaged"—meaning more importing, exporting, investing abroad, or connecting to inward investors—show themselves to be the most successful participants in declining sectors. Across sectors, whether expanding or contracting, the superior benefits associated with globally engaged firms accrue to average-skilled as well as high-skilled workers, to union members as well as nonunion workers, to those who live in small towns as well as large urban areas, and to minorities.

4

Globalization of R&D by US MNCs: Implications for US Prosperity

Public discussion and media reports about the National Science Foundation (NSF) report in 2012 on the global spread of research and development (R&D) used verbs that convey worry and concern. US companies are "shifting" laboratories to Asia. The US economy is "losing" R&D jobs. The US lead in science and technology is "rapidly shrinking." Other economies are "catching up." Asian nations are "matching" the United States in R&D investment. Engineering jobs that American multinational corporations are creating on campuses in India and China are "never coming back." Even the chairman of the NSF committee that produces the biennial report described the findings as "troubling."[1]

The NSF report mirrors publications from other entities—ranging from the Defense Science Board to the US-China Economic and Security Review Commission—in adopting a relentlessly zero-sum approach to both the location of R&D facilities and the distribution of benefits from R&D conducted abroad.

There are many reasons for the United States to want R&D expenditures of all MNCs (not just US MNCs) to take place in the United States. Direct benefits include breakthrough innovations, production process improvements, and quality advances for both goods and services in the US economy, accompanied by economies of scope and scale (clustering effects). Indirect benefits include spillovers in both horizontal and vertical directions—in other words, external benefits conferred on other firms, workers, and communities across America. High-paying jobs are present throughout.

---

1. See the chairman's comment in the press release for the 2012 report at www.nsf.gov/news/news_summ.jsp?cntn_id=122859 (accessed on March 25, 2013).

The contemporary debate about the globalization of R&D expenditures by US MNCs, however, involves the same two implicit assumptions that were explored in the previous chapter about production, exports, and capital expenditures. The first assumption, once again, is that external R&D expenditures by US multinational firms substitute for domestic R&D expenditures. The second is that greater amounts of R&D activity abroad confer little benefit to the United States and might actually undermine US prosperity.

Since these assumptions are almost taken as given, there has not been much acknowledgment or investigation of the idea that external R&D expenditures may complement and support domestic R&D and production activity. Nor is there much recognition that new laboratories, R&D campuses, and engineering graduates abroad (whether in Germany and Great Britain or India and China) can help to raise living standards in the United States. Nowhere is attention devoted to the appropriate counterfactual scenario.

This chapter offers a novel framework for analysis and policy recommendations. Other than enhancement of specific military capabilities, do stronger R&D capabilities in other countries damage the United States? How might the expansion of R&D activities abroad, including the training of large numbers of engineers and scientists, help raise living standards in the United States?

This chapter once again makes extensive analysis of Bureau of Economic Analysis (BEA) data. It also includes detailed case studies that might be particularly useful in painting a picture different from the zero-sum conceptualization of R&D that predominates in casual discussion of globalization.

The case studies provide practical examples showing that global R&D expenditures and operations of US MNCs may create complementary capabilities and interdependent competencies, rather than simply displacing one capability or competency from location A to location B. One example is General Electric Healthcare's Magnetic Resonance Imaging Laboratory team operating between the Niskayuna, New York campus, and the Munich, Germany, campus. The team jointly operates four whole-body scanners that have created major innovations in magnetic resonance imaging (MRI), allowing exceptional anatomic investigation involving the brain, spine, and musculoskeletal system. The synergy between the two research centers has generated spillovers that flow back to the United States. GE's Munich labs provided the initial insights that led to 32-channel, then 64-channel, then 128-channel imaging. This research is now incorporated into the high-end premium MRI equipment that is designed and built in the United States.

It may seem counterintuitive that the creation of new offshore R&D facilities could increase the amount of R&D carried out in the United States, but that is what case studies sometimes show. The creation of an R&D campus in Chennai, India, has allowed Caterpillar to create a 24-hour R&D cycle on engine propulsion and pollution control. The capital-intensive Caterpillar engine labs in Peoria, Illinois, operate two shifts with hundreds of channels of temperature, pressure, and emissions data to map diesel performance and emissions. These streams are sent overnight to Chennai, where the data are analyzed and returned to Peoria ready for the US engineers when they come to work the next morning. The chief technology officer of Caterpillar points out that the cost for the engine tests would be much greater if Caterpillar instead had a third shift working in the United States, making the company's overall R&D process less efficient and leaving less room for US engineers to exercise their comparative advantage. Using the growing Indian talent pool affects US operations positively by increasing the through-put and lowering the cost of the asset-intensive US test facilities. Round-the-clock interactions between Caterpillar's Indian and US test facilities help ensure the company's international market leadership position, while enabling headquarters to hire more US engineers.

Another discovery from the case studies is that the establishment of R&D facilities outside the United States may stimulate the development of goods and services for markets that do not have the same characteristics as the US market, enabling US MNCs to gain market share in those non-US markets. Caterpillar engineers in Chennai observed that the Indian market demanded a variant of the backhoe loader called a side-shift loader. The Chennai center carried out the design work for the side-shift loader, which is now sold around the world, although more in developing countries and in the European Union than in the United States (where this design is seldom used).

GE Healthcare engineers working on high-end electrocardiogram (ECG) systems in India were eager to create a product that was designed and priced for use across the wider Indian population—that is, an ECG machine that matched the economic and infrastructural realities of the country. They designed an ECG machine for a largely rural and poor population. The result is highly portable, can be easily carried to a patient's home, has a two-button operation that makes training faster, and can operate on battery in villages where the electricity supply is not dependable. This portable ECG machine costs a fraction of the high-end machine, with very little reduction in capability for most uses.

These case studies are consistent with emerging theoretical and empirical evidence on FDI by US firms. New trade and investment analyses of firm behavior at the micro level can shed light on the location of R&D capabilities. The predominant benefits from international trade and investment flows come not just from slow-moving, one-time shifts in comparative advantage according to inherent factor endowments. Rather, the benefits also come from sorting and shifting within individual firms and industries in response to competitive pressures for innovation and cost reduction. How does this phenomenon—widespread across inputs, final products, and finance—affect the analysis of R&D location?

Recent theories of MNC production have moved away from broad characteristics of countries and industries to instead focus on the division of labor within a firm and across borders. Management innovations and technological developments have made it increasingly feasible, and in many cases optimal, for firms to divide production into a series of tasks and then perform different tasks in different countries.

In these new understandings of how FDI operates, investment responds to the cost of separating tasks across borders, which in turn depends on technology, the relative need for production teams to be co-located in the same physical area, the skills and abilities of workers, the institutions of the countries in which production occurs, and the overall productivity level of the firm.[2]

These more sophisticated perspectives on FDI do not negate the importance of comparative advantage. Instead, they focus on a more nuanced concept of comparative advantage that can occur within firms as well as across countries and between different tasks required for the production of a single good or service rather than exclusively at the level of final products. In traditional models, comparative advantage arose from relatively static endowments of conventional factors such as land, labor, and capital. In today's more dynamic global environment, comparative advantage comes from relative strength in performing individual tasks. In the case of R&D, more abstract concepts—such as intellectual property protection, the ability of firms to innovate, and the capacity of workers to think creatively and solve problems—all contribute to comparative advantage not just across countries but also across firms.[3]

Even within the broad category of R&D, it is still possible for firms to exploit dynamic gains and increase their overall productivity by dividing R&D tasks across borders. For example, Lee Branstetter and C. Fritz Foley (2010) used patent data to study the R&D conducted by US firms in China and discovered that the activities performed there were very different from those that took place in the United States. First, patent activity in China is very low. In 2006, only 120 US firms had been granted patents for which at least one of the inventors was located in China. Of those US firms that had patenting activity in China, only about 1 percent of their annual patenting activity in 2006 took place in China. In addition, value added by Chinese affiliates of US firms continues to be very low. Together, these patterns suggest that the US-based activities consisted of high-value knowledge generation and the creation of new products. By contrast, R&D in China was more focused on development than on research and consisted primarily of tweaking existing designs so that they were suitable for production in Chinese factories and for sale in markets outside the United States.

Data from the BEA can help illustrate how these forces play out for US MNCs. Figure 4.1 tracks the R&D spending by US MNCs, both at home and abroad, from 1997 to 2010. The amount of R&D performed at foreign affiliates of US firms increased by $25 billion over this period. Yet spending on R&D by these firms inside the United States increased by $106 billion over the same time span. R&D spending in the United States still accounts for about 84 percent

---

2. See Baldwin and Robert-Nicoud (2010); Grossman and Rossi-Hansberg (2008); Antras, Garicano, and Rossi-Hansberg (2006); Markusen (2006); and Leamer and Storper (2001).

3. See Antras, Garicano, and Rossi-Hansberg (2006); Levchenko (2007); and Oldenski (2012).

Figure 4.1 R&D by US MNCs at home and abroad, 1997–2010

billions of dollars

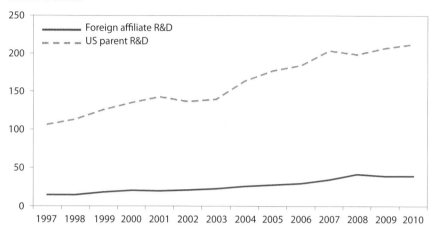

Note: Data are for nonbank US parents and nonbank majority-owned affiliates of US firms. Figures for 2010 are based on preliminary data releases.

Source: Bureau of Economic Analysis, www.bea.gov.

of total global R&D spending by US MNCs. This pattern suggests that while R&D spending has increased at foreign affiliates, MNCs still perform the vast majority of high-skilled activities in the United States.

The globalization of R&D by US MNCs has been a source of concern above and beyond overall multinational expansion. Because R&D is a high-skilled activity, its global expansion has been viewed by some as a sign that outward investment by US MNCs is moving away from low-skilled assembly work into areas where US workers have traditionally enjoyed a comparative advantage. Yet the expansion of R&D at foreign affiliates is also associated with positive employment and production outcomes for US workers.

Figure 4.2 shows the results of the empirical analysis described in chapter 3 as it applies to R&D performed by US MNCs at their foreign affiliates. Foreign expansion of R&D is still small (figure 4.1), but it is positively and significantly associated with the expansion of R&D, capital expenditures, exports, sales, and employment in the United States. As with other activities of MNCs, outward expansion of R&D is a complement to, not a substitute for, domestic activities.

What is also striking in the data is the discovery that firms that do not increase their R&D abroad do not increase it at home, either. It is not possible to know the true counterfactual. However, because this analysis looks at changes over time within each firm, the evidence suggests that if US MNCs were to reduce their foreign R&D due to policy restrictions or other factors, then R&D, capital expenditures, exports, sales, and employment in the United States would likely fall as well.

Figure 4.2   Greater foreign expansion of R&D is associated with increased domestic activities of US MNCs

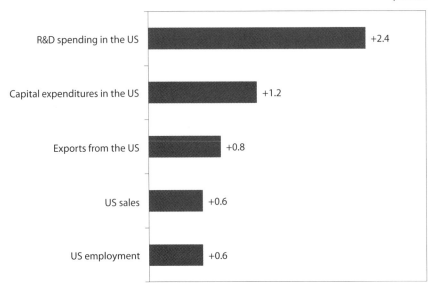

Note: All results are statistically significant at the 1 percent level. See appendix A for a more detailed regression table.

Source: Based on regressions using firm-level data for 1990–2009 from the Bureau of Economic Analysis, www.bea.gov.

The following three case studies illustrate the kinds of complementarities that are captured within the aggregate data. They benefit from access to internal data and highest-level technology management in Caterpillar and GE Healthcare, but they cannot be assumed to be representative of all other US MNCs.

Case Study 1: Caterpillar's Next-Generation Power Trains and Engine Emissions and Efficiency[4]

With 2011 sales and revenues of $60.1 billion, Caterpillar is the world's leading manufacturer of construction and mining equipment, diesel and natural gas engines, industrial gas turbines, and diesel-electric locomotives. R&D at Caterpillar is the means by which the company identifies, creates, and perfects the technologies and solutions that help its customers be successful. R&D is

---

4. The authors thank Tana Utley, Caterpillar's vice president and chief technology officer, and her staff for help with the materials upon which this case study is based.

powered by the Caterpillar engineering community of more than 8,000 highly skilled technical experts around the world, including 250 PhD-level scientists and engineers.

Caterpillar divides R&D into three principal categories. The first is applied research on products that are typically one new cycle away from introduction (usually 5 to 10 years). This category also includes the development of new engineering tools. The second is new product introduction, which can be an incremental improvement to an existing product or a new offering that provides improved features and benefits to the customer. The third category is continuous product improvement, which is oriented toward improving reliability in existing products.

Caterpillar business units have decision making rights regarding spending on new product introduction and continuous product improvement, aligning how much they want to spend on incremental improvement and on improving reliability of existing products with the market goals of their unit. Caterpillar's chief technology officer is the corporation's overall decision maker for applied research on next-cycle products that are 5 to 10 years from the market.

Two of the most important categories of Caterpillar R&D are next-generation power trains and engine emissions and efficiency. Looking to the future, hybrid technology is a category of growing interest.

Power trains provide and transmit the power required to propel machines from place to place. Primary power is normally provided by an internal combustion engine followed by a variety of "power transmitters" constituting the drivetrain. These may include planetary or countershaft mechanical transmissions, continuously variable transmissions, hydraulic pumps and motors, electric generators and motors, differentials, axles, and final drives. How Caterpillar configures these components is determined by how the machine will be used and what the customers require for their business success. These parameters inform power train research—how to minimize the cost of performing the work by reducing efficiency losses while improving reliability, durability, and performance.

Engine research at Caterpillar is focused on increasing the efficiency of the diesel engine to address robustness to fuel variations, low emissions, fuel efficiency, low product cost, suitability to world markets, durability, and reliability. Caterpillar researchers continue to evolve the basic building blocks of combustion processes, fuel systems, air systems, electronics, and after-treatment, while pursuing the increased-value opportunities that come with integration of these elements into system solutions. In addition, Caterpillar continues to design and develop advanced engines, including higher cylinder pressures, increased engine rating capability, and lower cost.

Caterpillar has R&D Proving Grounds in Peoria, Illinois, and Ono, Japan. The company has an engine development lab in the United Kingdom and does engine design work in Germany, the United Kingdom, and the United States. These facilities are complemented by an Engineering Design Center in Chennai, India, and an R&D Center in Wuxi, China. The hands-on skills of university graduates in India and China are poorer than their developed-world counterparts. Chinese and Indian universities may not be placing sufficient emphasis on teamwork and independent initiative, so Caterpillar has developed special training programs to supplement these skills and enable these engineers to make a larger contribution to the company's R&D base.

The R&D Center in Wuxi, China, supports market share growth in China as well as sales of Caterpillar products in Asia. The challenges of protecting intellectual property in China will ultimately adversely impact the company's ability to do more R&D there.

The Engineering Design Center in Chennai originally exploited the trade-off between cost and quality, using less-expensive Indian technicians to do less-sophisticated engineering services. Over time, the center has outsourced the less-sophisticated work to other Indian firms while raising the skill level of the center's personnel. Caterpillar rotates US R&D personnel through 3- to 12-month training assignments abroad and also deploys US trainers and facilitators at overseas operations. It should be noted that what Caterpillar calls its "international service employees" are extremely expensive, since they require relocating a US citizen abroad with a significant pay premium, plus coverage of housing and sometimes family expenses such as education allowances for children.

A particularly valuable contribution from the Chennai facility is overnight processing to complement the activities of Caterpillar's R&D in the United States, allowing a 24/7 R&D cycle within the company. The capital-intensive engine lab in Peoria may operate two shifts with hundreds of channels of temperature, pressure, and emissions data to map diesel performance and emissions. These streams are sent overnight to Chennai, where the data are analyzed and returned to Peoria ready for US engineers when they come to work the next morning. The cost for the engine tests would be much greater if Caterpillar instead were to have a third shift working in the United States, which would make the company's overall R&D process less efficient and leave less room for US engineers to exercise their comparative advantage. Use of the growing Indian talent pool affects Caterpillar's US operations quite positively by increasing the through-put and lowering the cost of the asset-intensive US test facilities. The round-the-clock interactions between Caterpillar's Indian and US test facilities help ensure the company's international market leadership position, thus enabling its headquarters to hire more US engineers.

The Chennai facility now does more sophisticated engineering work that does not need to be done next to the supply or consumer base. This work includes higher-end analysis and design work for Caterpillar equipment. Some product innovation carried out in Chennai is beginning to affect US-based designs. A low-cost but sturdy implement built for the Indian market is now being incorporated into US-made equipment. The Chennai campus has also become a "Center of Excellence" for time-intensive computer simulation of how to design a new plant or how to retool a new line for a new machine, regardless of where Caterpillar might ultimately locate the new plant or the retooled line, including back in the United States.

Table 4.1 Caterpillar's R&D expenses and spending, 2007–11

Year	Total R&D expenses (millions of dollars)	R&D spending (percent of total revenue)
2007	1,404	3.1
2008	1,728	3.4
2009	1,421	4.4
2010	1,905	4.5
2011	2,297	4.0

Source: Caterpillar, Inc., www.caterpillar.com.

Similarly, when the Indian market demanded a variant of the backhoe loader called a side-shift loader, the Chennai center conducted the design work. The side-shift loader is now sold around the world, though more in developing countries and in the European Union than in the United States.

Table 4.1 shows Caterpillar's aggregate R&D spending from 2007 to 2011. In terms of the distribution of R&D personnel, in 2012 Caterpillar had some 8,500 degree-holding engineers, including approximately 1,000 in India and 700 in China.

Case Study 2: General Electric Healthcare's Diagnostic Imaging Business[5]

General Electric has five Global Research Centers: the global headquarters of GE Global Research in Niskayuna, New York; the Center for GE Global Research-Europe near Munich, Germany; the John F. Welch Technology Center in Bangalore, India; the China Technology Center in Shanghai; and the Multidisciplinary Research and Development Center under construction in Rio de Janeiro, Brazil. The Global Research Centers are multi-industry and multidisciplinary, with competencies that range from aerothermal research to advanced materials, electrical and chemical engineering, software development, and healthcare R&D.

General Electric spent between $3.1 billion and $4.6 billion on R&D annually between 2008 and 2011 (table 4.2). Included among those totals, GE Healthcare alone spent approximately $800 million on R&D each year.

One of GE Healthcare's most successful and competitive product areas involves diagnostic imaging technologies that include MRI systems. MRI equipment not only gives doctors and researchers a far higher resolution than

5. The authors thank Mike Harsh, GE Healthcare vice president and chief technology officer, and his associates for providing the materials upon which this case study is based. The General Electric Foundation partially supported the research underlying this volume.

Table 4.2 Evolution of General Electric's aggregate spending on R&D, 2008–11

Year	Billions of dollars
2008	3.1
2009	3.3
2010	3.9
2011	4.6

Source: General Electric, www.ge.com.

traditional X-rays but also provides three-dimensional cross-sectional images that can significantly reduce the need for exploratory surgery and its attendant risks. MRI capabilities have also changed the way physicians and researchers follow cancers and the response of cancers to therapy.

GE Healthcare's Magnetic Resonance Imaging Laboratory team operates three 1.5 tesla scanner and one 3.0 tesla whole-body scanner in the Niskayuna, New York, and Munich, Germany, campuses. Tesla is the unit of measurement quantifying the strength of a magnetic field. MRI signals are extremely weak because they emanate from a relatively small number of protons. A key objective is to maximize the signal-to-noise ratio, which is dependent on a number of fundamental parameters such as in-plane resolution, number of excitations (or signal averages), proximity of receiver coils, and field strength. The first 1.5 tesla whole-body scanner with a high enough signal-to-noise ratio to be effective was developed in Global Research's MRI lab in Niskayuna in 1983. This revolutionary breakthrough has been followed by major innovations in magnetic resonance, including phased array coils, folded gradient coils, phase contrast imaging, and 32-channel and 128-channel receiver systems. Today the MRI team operating in Niskayuna and Munich is able to uncover exceptional anatomic detail that allows assessment of pathological conditions involving the brain, spine, and musculoskeletal system.

Assembling the base for GE's success in diagnostic imaging techniques such as MRI systems and hardware has involved both internal expansion and external acquisition. For example, GE Healthcare's first US MRI plant in Waukesha, Wisconsin, in 1983 required an investment of nearly $10 billion, with construction of a separate facility to produce GE's own magnets shortly thereafter. Much of GE Healthcare's expansion, however, was built upon acquisitions of operating companies, allowing GE Healthcare to take advantage of their products and production expertise, as well as their scientists, engineers, and patents. In 1985, GE acquired a company called Technicare that produced a variety of X-ray diagnostic equipment from Johnson and Johnson. To expand its ultrasound imaging capabilities, GE Healthcare bought Diasonics Vingmed from Elbit Medical Imaging in Haifa, Israel, in 1998.

Soon thereafter GE Healthcare undertook two major expansions in Europe, one through acquisition, the other through direct investment in a new Global Research Center. In 2004, GE Healthcare acquired UK-based Amersham plc for $9 billion. Amersham had its origins in the UK Atomic Energy Authority for the development and manufacturing of radioactive materials for peacetime uses. It was the first company to be privatized by the UK government under Prime Minister Margaret Thatcher, and it developed formidable capabilities in medical diagnostics (among other healthcare fields) that nicely complemented what was then known as GE Medical's strengths in this field. Sir William Castell, former CEO of Amersham, became CEO of GE Healthcare, and GE Healthcare's global headquarters was established in Chalfont St. Giles, Buckinghamshire in the United Kingdom, where it remains to this day.

Also in 2004, the GE parent began to build its European Global Research Center alongside the Garching campus of the Technical University of Munich (*Technische Universität München*). As a world-class industrial lab in a university setting, the center employs approximately 150 scientists and technologists from more than 20 countries in disciplines that include chemistry, physics, mathematics, engineering, and materials research. Medical R&D is but one component of the center's activities, but it has become a pole of the work of the Niskayuna-Munich MRI team. Medical R&D has also specialized in development of advanced clinical applications for ultrasound and computed tomography as well as magnetic resonance. The Munich center provided the initial insights that led to 32-channel, then 64-channel, then 128-channel MRI. This research is now incorporated into high-end premium MRI equipment that is designed and built in the United States.

Performing MRI R&D in Germany—as in the former-Amersham facilities in the United Kingdom—allows for close monitoring of new developments in the backyard of GE Healthcare's most formidable competitors in medical diagnostic imaging, Siemens and Philips.

GE Healthcare sales of diagnostic and clinical equipment was approximately $7.8 billion in 2011, and 53 percent of total revenue comes from outside the United States. This places GE Healthcare consistently in first or second place in comparison to Siemens and Philips.

An important spillover from GE's success in MRI is now evidenced in the use of GE Healthcare's MRI magnet technology in a completely different business category—to cost-effectively scale up to 10 to 15 megawatt wind turbines. Today, most wind turbines have conventional generators that are connected to a gearbox. The gearbox is used to step up lower blade speeds into higher speeds so as to reduce the torque requirements before it reaches the generator. This means higher costs in scaling up to larger wind platforms because of additional weight and maintenance needs that will be required.

The key challenge will be to deliver new technologies that achieve the right scale and cost in the development of higher megawatt machines to maximize clean wind power opportunities around the globe. Applying its more than 30 years of experience with superconducting magnets for MRI systems in healthcare, GE is developing an innovative new generator technology that will deliver more power while helping reduce the cost of wind power. GE is applying superconducting magnets to make lower-cost systems with higher image quality with the goal of enabling wind turbines to generate more wind power at a lower cost of electricity. GE was awarded a two-year $3 million grant from the US Department of Energy in 2011 to develop a next-generation wind turbine generator that could support large-scale wind applications in the 10 to 15 megawatt range.

Incorporating a GE Healthcare innovation like superconducting magnets into a novel application elsewhere in GE product offerings is not limited to wind turbines. GE breakthroughs in medical picture archiving—running to thousands of images—are now used for storing, analyzing, and inspecting digital snapshots of train engine parts, turbine blades, and pipeline segments. Similarly, computer visualization first developed in medical MRI systems was reoriented toward NBC sports, showing the quarterback's view of how a pass play was developing downfield.

Finally, GE researchers in the United States, Germany, India, and Brazil recognized that they faced a similar challenge in monitoring very large real-time data streaming from airplane avionics, smart-grid electrical systems, and medical imaging. At GE's software lab in San Ramon, California, an engineering vice president hired away from Cisco developed a system-of-systems diagnostic technique to identify when multiple terabytes of data veer outside the normal envelope of operation.

Case Study 3: General Electric Healthcare's "Reverse Innovation" in India

Former GE Professor in Residence and Chief Innovation Consultant Vijay Govindarajan has noted that in the history of modern medical technology, most products have been developed in and for markets that are most able to afford them and then modified later for distribution in other areas (Govindarajan and Trimble 2012).[6] From a business perspective, it seems perfectly logical to market the new products first in the United States and Europe. But in practice this has meant that many life-saving tools and procedures have been slow to trickle through to developing countries beyond their major medical centers.

Across large swathes of the developing world, not to mention some parts of developed countries, there is simply no economic means to equip clinics and general practitioners with advanced medical equipment. Poor infrastructure can impede the use of high-end medical equipment, as electrical supplies are often unreliable in many areas and poor roads or public transportation can make it difficult for people to access the care they need. Shortages of trained medical staff are also a huge problem. Skilled doctors and nurses often move to

---

6. Govindarajan worked for GE in 2010–11. He is currently a professor of international business at the Tuck School of Business at Dartmouth College.

urban centers or migrate to earn a better living, leaving rural areas underserved. In India, for example, 75 percent of medical professionals work in urban centers, leaving only 25 percent to serve three-quarters of the country's population.

All of these factors affect how healthcare is delivered in any particular market, and they underscore the weaknesses of simply pushing developed technologies to the developing world.

At GE Healthcare, the traditional model of product development has been gradually shifting toward in-market innovation—that is, designing entirely new products to meet the needs of a specific country or region. GE Healthcare's MAC line of ECG systems, for example, is a success story of innovation for India and the world.

The ECG is the most widely performed cardiac test in the developed world, and GE has long been at the forefront of the industry. GE's traditional approach has been to market high-end ECG systems for major hospitals in urban centers in India. But by 2005, GE's engineers in India were eager to create a product that was designed and priced for use across the wider Indian population—an ECG machine that would reflect the economic and infrastructural realities of the country. What emerged in 2007 was the MAC 400, an ECG machine designed to extend the capability of traditional ECGs to a largely rural and poor population. The MAC 400 is highly portable and can be easily carried to a patient's home, has an easy two-button operation that makes training faster, and can operate on battery. Above all, the MAC 400 costs around $800, compared with other hospital-class units from GE Healthcare that range from $2,000 to $10,000.

Carrying their efforts even further, the GE Healthcare team at the John F. Welch Technology Center in Bangalore, one of GE's largest integrated multidisciplinary R&D centers, set a new bar for low-cost ECGs in 2011 with the MAC India. Incorporating a smaller printer and battery-only use, the MAC India is priced at $500, potentially reducing the cost of a single ECG exam to as little as the price of a bottle of water for rural patients. Moreover, battery performance has been enhanced, enabling as many as 500 ECG readings on a single battery charge.

Another innovation followed—digitizing the entire process in order to take into account the gap in skilled manpower as well as accessibility issues involved in using the machines in large cardiac camps or reaching patients in inaccessible areas. The MAC 600 was developed with a built-in screen to view ECGs instantly, eliminating the need to print all ECGs and thereby saving cost and paper. The MAC 600 also allows technicians and doctors to store and transfer ECGs in a universal portable digital format (PDF) using any multimedia phone.

GE Healthcare's Bangalore team recently introduced the variant of the ECG machine at half the price of the MAC 400. The new MACs incorporate the Marquette 12SL analysis program, which is standard in GE's premium ECG devices, and include built-in software that interprets the ECG in English like any pathological test, a feature that previously was available only in very high-end ECG machines.

Govindarajan calls GE Healthcare's strategy "reverse innovation," and, indeed, over the past three years, approximately 60 percent of sales of the MAC 400 and 600 have been in developing countries, including India, Latin America, and China. He points out that historically, innovations have always happened in rich countries. But in the future, innovations will have to take place in countries like India and China, because that is where the bulk of the customers are. The needs are more pressing there and the sheer volumes will justify the investments that will be required for developing the appropriate products.

Observations from Case Studies

The discovery of complementarity in the aggregate data between external R&D and US home-country R&D within US multinational firms may seem counterintuitive to many. These case studies may therefore be particularly useful in painting a picture of how such complementarity manifests itself (and how it can produce positive results).

Within the case studies, global R&D expenditures and operations of these US MNCs create complementary capabilities and interdependent competencies, rather than simply displacing one capability or competency from one location to another. GE's MRI Laboratory team operating cooperatively between the Niskayuna, New York, and Munich, Germany, campuses is one example. For Caterpillar, the campus in Chennai, India, allows overnight processing to complement the activities of its R&D in the United States, facilitating a 24/7 R&D cycle. The cost for the engine tests would be much greater if Caterpillar instead were to have a third shift working in the United States, which would make the company's overall R&D process less efficient and in turn constrain Caterpillar from hiring more engineers in the United States. For these multinational investors, overseas R&D facilities also bring spillover back to the United States. GE Healthcare research on superconducting magnets for MRI in Germany and the United States allowed the GE parent in the United States to develop more efficient power systems for wind turbines. GE's Munich Global Research Center provided the initial insights that led to 32-channel, then 64-channel, then 128-channel MRI. This research is now incorporated into the high-end premium MRI equipment designed and built in the United States. A low-cost but sturdy excavator-implement that Caterpillar designed in Chennai for the Indian market is now being incorporated into US-made digging equipment.

What is conventionally thought of as R&D may be carried out simply by building new or bigger laboratories. But often the process is built upon acquisition of other companies, including of course those companies' products and production expertise as well as their scientists, engineers, and patents. After GE Healthcare acquired UK-based Amersham to enhance GE's capabilities in medical diagnostics (among other healthcare fields), Sir William Castell, former CEO of Amersham, became CEO of GE Healthcare, and GE Healthcare's global headquarters was established in Calfont St. Giles, Buckinghamshire.

Overseas research facilities also offer a view on new R&D taking place in other countries as well as surveillance of what competitors are doing. GE's R&D location for MRI in Germany allows for close monitoring of new developments in the backyard to GE Healthcare's most formidable competitors in medical diagnostic imaging, Siemens and Philips.

Finally, the case studies show that the establishment of R&D facilities outside the United States may stimulate the development of goods and services for markets that do not have the same characteristics as the US market, enabling US MNCs to gain market share in those non-US markets. The Caterpillar engineers in Chennai observed that the Indian market demanded a variant of the backhoe loader called a side-shift loader. The Chennai center carried out the design work for the side-shift loader, which is now sold around the world, but more in developing countries and in the European Union than in the United States (where this design is seldom used). GE Healthcare engineers working on high-end ECG systems in India were eager to create an ECG machine designed and priced for use across the wider Indian population. They designed an ECG machine to extend the capability of traditional ECG to a largely rural and poor population. The resulting ECG machine is highly portable and can be easily carried to a patient's home, has an easy two-button operation that makes training faster, and can operate on battery. It costs a fraction of the high-end ECG with very little reduction in capability for most uses.

5

Tax Policy toward Multinational Corporations

Tax policy attracted maximum attention in the closing hours of 2012 and seems likely to attract more attention in the 113th US Congress in 2013. The immediate reason was the "fiscal cliff" that affected scores of tax relief provisions as well as defense and discretionary domestic spending and the fact that the cliff was not entirely resolved in the December 2012 "lame duck" session of Congress. The way the fiscal cliff was structured, multiple tax relief provisions were destined to expire and domestic spending was scheduled to be slashed starting January 1, 2013, unless Congress said otherwise. Congress did say otherwise, mainly postponing hard decisions and doing very little to eliminate the specter of growing federal deficits and a rising debt-to-GDP ratio. The prospects are stark: Under current policy, average annual deficits will exceed 5 percent of GDP for the next decade, and the ratio of debt held by the public to GDP will rise to exceed 90 percent of GDP in 2022.

By raising taxes on those deemed rich (households with income above $450,000 annually), and by restoring the payroll tax on individuals to its normal rate of 6.2 percent, Congress raised an estimated $620 billion in revenue over the next 10 years. But this is far from adequate. Moreover, decisions on domestic spending were rolled over to March 2013 and beyond, so a series of "fiscal gorges" now await presidential and congressional action.

So far, the congressional debate has centered on individual income tax provisions, especially the relative burdens on what are being defined as rich and middle-class taxpayers, with the above-mentioned $450,000 being the most recent dividing line. But corporate taxation will not be forgotten in 2013, and within the corporate tax arena a fair amount of attention will be given to MNCs. That is both a concern and an opportunity, particularly since reform is so badly needed.

Complementarities Are the Key

The central message from the new research for this study, as well as from the prior research by others, is simple and powerful: Outward foreign direct investment (FDI) is not a substitute but rather a complement to the US economy. Better jobs, higher investment, larger exports, and more R&D go hand-in-hand with greater outward FDI. Unfortunately, much of the recent debate over corporate tax policy reflects a zero-sum view of MNC activity.[1] According to this view, more investment abroad means less investment in the United States. More jobs abroad mean fewer jobs at home. And so on.

Building on a zero-sum view, some observers call for tightening US tax rules on foreign earnings, even to the extent of taxing all foreign earnings currently at the US statutory rate. This "reform" is supposed to prompt MNCs to ramp up US investment and create more jobs at home. Our analysis suggests that the prescription is exactly wrong. Since Congress has thus far declined to enact proposed reforms of this nature, we cannot be absolutely certain that imposing higher US taxes on the foreign earnings of US MNCs would diminish their appetite for investment abroad or curtail their R&D and employment at home. But strong complementarities between outward FDI and jobs, investment, and R&D in the US economy suggest that such an initiative would undermine US prosperity.

Excessive Corporate Taxation

The backdrop of the debate over MNC taxation is a US corporate tax rate that has gotten completely out of line with world practice. During the 1990s, the US corporate tax position steadily worsened among its competitors in the Organization for Economic Cooperation and Development (OECD). In 1985, the United States ranked ninth among 19 countries (meaning US rates were higher than eight other OECD countries and lower than 10 other). By 1995, despite reforms in 1986 under the Ronald Reagan administration, the United States ranked 12th because other countries cut their corporate rates more. By 2003, the United States ranked 17th (Hufbauer and Grieco 2005). By 2012, Japan and Germany had cut their statutory corporate tax rates, leaving the United States as the highest corporate tax country within the OECD, and thereby earning the lowest ranking. Meanwhile, the 2000s saw the ascent of the BRICS bloc of countries (Brazil, Russia, India, China, and South Africa) as industrial powerhouses, sometimes spurred by special concessions leading to very low effective corporate tax rates.

The US statutory corporate tax rate (federal and state combined) is now 39 percent. This is 11 percentage points higher than the unweighted average of competing countries. However, it is not just the statutory tax rate that makes

---

1. A leading proponent of the zero-sum view when unemployment is high is Clausing (2012a, 2012b). See the response and rejoinder by Hufbauer (2012a, 2012b).

the United States unfriendly to business. The US average effective tax rate (again federal and state) and the US marginal effective corporate tax rate are also among the highest worldwide. As shown in table 5.1, the US average effective tax rate is 8 to 9 percentage points higher than the unweighted average of competing countries, and the US marginal effective tax rate is 3 to 11 percentage points higher.

The fact that the US Treasury does not collect a particularly large share of revenue from corporate taxation (typically under 3 percent of GDP) reflects the reality that around half of US business activity is conducted by "pass-through" entities (partnerships, limited liability companies, Subchapter S corporations, etc.) that do not pay corporate tax.[2] On the other hand, large firms, including US MNCs, are fully subject to high US corporate tax rates, however measured.

As discussed later in this chapter, research by Harry G. Grubert (2012) strongly indicates that US MNCs are able to lower the rate of return on domestic sales and raise the rate of return on foreign sales by creative transfer pricing between related affiliates. By shifting reported profits to jurisdictions that impose lower corporate tax rates, MNCs reduce their US tax burden. Contrary to other scholars, however, we regard this phenomenon as a useful escape valve from the burdensome US corporate tax structure.

The United States still insists on the formal structure of worldwide taxation, meaning that US MNCs are theoretically subject to US taxation, at the high statutory rate, on the worldwide income of all their foreign affiliates. In practice, flexible features of complex international tax law allow MNCs to pay lower rates (in line with their foreign competitors). Most importantly, US parent companies of MNC groups can defer the repatriation of earnings from their subsidiaries abroad and thereby delay—perhaps permanently—the payment of high US corporate taxes. However, the formal structure of worldwide taxation is often used as a springboard for proposed "reforms" that would sharply increase the tax burden on foreign earnings. By contrast, most other countries practice territorial taxation, meaning that foreign affiliates pay a sharply reduced (or zero) rate of taxation to the home country on their active business income.

In the words of the Simpson-Bowles Commission report (p. 28):[3]

> The corporate income tax, meanwhile, hurts America's ability to compete. On the one hand, statutory rates in the U.S. are significantly higher than the average for industrialized countries (even as revenue collection is low), and our method of taxing foreign income is outside the norm. The U.S. is one of the only industrialized countries with a hybrid system of taxing active foreign-source income. The current system puts U.S. corporations at a competitive disadvantage against their foreign competitors. A territorial tax system should be adopted to help put the U.S. system in line with other countries, leveling the playing field.

---

2. See Auerbach (2006) for a detailed examination of the forces, including the rise of pass-through entities, that explain the modest share of GDP collected in corporate taxes.

3. The White House, *Report of The National Commission on Fiscal Responsibility and Reform: The Moment of Truth*, December 2010, www.fiscalcommission.gov/sites/fiscalcommission.gov/files/documents/TheMomentofTruth12_1_2010.pdf (accessed on March 25, 2013).

Table 5.1   Statutory, average, and marginal effective corporate tax rates for systemically important countries (percent)

Country	Statutory corporate tax rate, 2010[a] (OECD tax database (2011))	Average effective corporate tax rate[b]		Marginal effective corporate tax rate, 2010[c]	
		2009 (World Bank, PwC, and IFC 2010)	2010 (Hassett and Mathur 2011)	Chen and Mintz (2012)	Hassett and Mathur (2011)
Australia[d]	30.0	25.9	22.2	26.0	17.0
Brazil[e]	34.0	21.4	n.a.	35.1	n.a.
Canada	29.5	9.8	25.5	20.5	23.4
China[f]	25.0	6.0	n.a.	16.6	n.a.
France[g]	34.4	8.2	27.5	34.0	23.8
Germany[h]	30.2	22.9	24.2	23.8	20.7
India[i]	34.0	24.0	n.a.	33.6	n.a.
Italy[j]	27.5	22.8	24.3	26.9	22.6
Japan	39.5	27.9	33.0	29.5	30.5
Korea	24.2	15.3	18.1	29.5	13.6
Mexico	30.0	23.1	28.4	17.5	27.7
Netherlands[k]	25.5	20.9	19.4	16.8	15.1
Poland[l]	19.0	17.7	16.2	14.3	14.1
Russia[m]	20.0	9.0	n.a.	31.9	n.a.
South Africa[n]	34.6	24.3	n.a.	14.5	n.a.
Spain	30.0	20.9	27.5	25.4	26.3

Sweden	26.3	16.4	18.5	18.9	12.6
Switzerland[o]	21.2	8.9	15.4	17.6	10.9
Turkey	20.0	17.0	13.1	5.6	7.3
United Kingdom[p]	28.0	23.2	22.3	27.9	18.8
United States[q]	39.2	27.6	29.0	34.6	23.6
Unweighted average, excluding United States[r]	28.1	18.3	21.0	23.3	20.8

n.a. = not available.

a. The statutory corporate tax rates for Organization for Economic Cooperation and Development (OECD) countries (all countries except Brazil, China, India, Russia, and South Africa) show the combined central and subcentral corporate income tax rates. The subcentral coverage of statutory corporate tax rates for non-OECD countries is not necessarily consistent.

b. The average effective corporate income tax rate measures the average rate a firm might expect to face on an investment project over the possible range of profitability outcomes. Hassett and Mathur (2011) calculated their average effective tax rates based on the approach outlined by Devereux and Griffith (1999).

c. The marginal effective corporate tax rate measures the tax liability incurred on an additional dollar of investment and informs scaling choices, conditional on the location. The Chen and Mintz (2012) marginal effective tax rates do not include the effects of the 100 percent temporary capital expensing or "bonus depreciation" rules passed by Congress in December 2010 in the Tax Relief, Unemployment Insurance Reauthorization, and Job Creation Act. This rule increased the 50 percent bonus depreciation in the tax code's section 168(k) to 100 percent for qualified property placed in service before December 2011. Chen and Mintz calculated that this provision reduces the US effective tax rate to as low as 17.5 percent, but only for a single year; it does not provide certainty for firms in their capital planning decisions, and it may simply accelerate investment outlays. For these reasons, Chen and Mintz excluded bonus depreciation effects in their marginal effective tax rate calculation. Hassett and Mathur (2011) calculated their marginal effective tax rates based on the approach outlined by Devereux and Griffith (1999).

d. Australia has a noncalendar tax year. Its statutory rates are in effect as of July 1.

e. The Brazilian statutory corporate income tax rate is 25 percent. In addition, social contributions on net profits are levied at a rate of 9 percent, leading to an overall rate of 34 percent. The 25 percent corporate income tax rate includes a 15 percent basic rate on net profits with tax adjustments and an additional income tax of 10 percent on the net profits that exceed 240,000 Brazilian real per year.

f. For statutory rates, as of January 2008 foreign and domestic entities are subject to a single enterprise corporate income tax at a rate of 25 percent. However, the rate for a low-profit enterprise is 20 percent, and for a high-tech enterprises the rate is 15 percent if certain conditions are met.

g. The French statutory rate includes a surcharge and does not include the local business tax (taxe professionnelle) or the turnover-based solidarity tax (contribution de solidarité).

h. The German statutory rate includes the regional trade tax (Gewerbesteuer) and the surcharge.

(continues on next page)

Table 5.1 Statutory, average, and marginal effective corporate tax rates for systemically important countries (percent) *(continued)*

i. For statutory rates, domestic companies are generally taxed at the rate of 30 percent; however, profits from life insurance business in India are taxed at a rate of 12.5 percent. Foreign companies are taxed at a rate of 40 percent. A minimum alternate tax (MAT) is levied at 15 percent of the adjusted profits of companies where the tax payable is less than 15 percent of their book profits. A dividend distribution tax (DDT) is levied at 15 percent on dividends distributed by a domestic company. Surcharge and education cess is applicable on the above taxes. A 10 percent surcharge in the case of domestic companies and a 2.5 percent surcharge in the case of foreign companies is applicable if total income is in excess of 10 million rupees. An education cess of 3 percent is applicable on income tax plus surcharge, if any. A wealth tax is imposed at a rate of 1 percent on the value of specified assets held by the taxpayer in excess of the basic exemption of 3 million rupees. A securities transaction tax is levied on the value of taxable securities transactions in equity shares and units of equity-oriented funds.

j. The Italian statutory rates do not include the regional business tax (*Imposta Regionale sulle Attività Produttive*—IRAP).

k. The Dutch statutory corporate tax rate applies to taxable income over 200,000 euros.

l. There is no Polish subcentral government statutory tax. However, local authorities (at each level) participate in tax revenue at a specified percentage for each level of local authority.

m. The statutory corporate income tax is split into the federal tax (2 percent) and the regional tax (18 percent that can be reduced to 13.5 percent for some categories of taxpayers). Dividends distributed can be subject to a 9 percent or 0 percent withholding tax. Interest income on state securities can be subject to a 15 percent or 0 percent withholding tax.

n. The statutory corporate income tax rate is 28 percent. However, South Africa imposes an additional secondary tax on companies (STC) at 10 percent on any net dividends declared by them. Therefore, if a company distributes 100 percent of its after-tax earnings as a dividend, an effective tax rate of 34.55 percent will apply. This does not apply to gold mining companies (which are taxed on a formula basis) or to South African branches of foreign entities, which are taxed at a rate of 33 percent. The STC may be replaced by a withholding tax in the future.

o. In Switzerland, church taxes cannot be avoided by enterprises. They are included in the statutory rates.

p. The United Kingdom has a noncalendar tax year. Its statutory rates are in effect as of April 1.

q. The US subcentral statutory corporate rate is a weighted average of state corporate marginal income tax rates. The US effective corporate rate excludes bonus depreciation.

r. Hassett and Mathur (2011) do not have the data for some countries in the table. Hence, the unweighted average calculated from their numbers supplements the missing cells with data from either Chen and Mintz (2012) or World Bank, PwC, and IFC (2010) to enable an estimate.

Sources: Corporate tax rates for OECD countries are from the OECD 2011 tax database, www.oecd.org/tax/tax-policy/oecdtaxdatabase.htm (accessed March 25, 2013). Corporate tax rates for non-OECD countries are from KPMG's 2010 Corporate and Indirect Tax Rate Survey, www.kpmg.com/Global/en/Pages/Default.aspx (accessed March 25, 2013). Marginal effective corporate tax rates are from Chen and Mintz (2012). Average effective corporate income taxes are from World Bank, PwC, and IFC (2010). Marginal and average effective corporate income taxes are from Hassett and Mathur (2011) and authors' calculations.

Two decades ago, when Gary Clyde Hufbauer and Joanna van Rooij (1992) first advocated a territorial tax system for the United States, theirs were lonely voices. Under a territorial system, profits earned by foreign subsidiaries abroad are not taxed at all by the home country or are taxed at a reduced rate (e.g., 10 percent). Today a majority of knowledgeable commentators, including the Simpson-Bowles Commission, favor some form of territorial tax system. To be sure, not everyone agrees: The Obama administration advocates much higher taxation of foreign income. On balance, however, arguments for competitive neutrality in world markets, for preserving the US role as a headquarters location for MNCs, and for tax simplification have shifted informed opinion toward territorial systems.

In years past, defenders of high corporate tax rates appealed to flexible exchange rates as the answer to international competition. According to this narrative, offsetting movements in exchange rates will wash away business tax differences, leaving "fundamental forces" to determine national investment, production, and exports. But for decades, the safe haven character of the US dollar has attracted a seemingly unlimited inflow of capital from foreign central banks and private investors, which in turn has long kept the dollar overvalued relative to other key currencies. Meanwhile, corporate decisions are fostering human skills and innovation and preparing the ground for future investments. Such decisions shape fundamental forces—that is, the basic competitive structure of the US economy is path-determined by prior corporate investment, research, and on-the-job worker training patterns. Long before dollar depreciation will convincingly offset high corporate tax rates, mobile MNCs will choose to invest elsewhere, and in doing so put the United States at a permanent disadvantage.

Underlying this danger are a large and expanding share of production that is mobile thanks to the Internet, rapid transportation, and the growing importance of high-tech goods and services with elevated value-to-weight ratios. Based on J. Bradford Jensen's (2011) calculations explained in appendix B, we estimate that 66 percent of US manufactured goods and 72 percent of US services are mobile. Together, these account for 69 percent of the private US economy. Additionally, we estimate that nearly half (46.5 percent) of US private-sector jobs are tradable. At the same time that this mobility of goods and tradability of jobs has increased, numerous countries have entered the comfort zone of market capitalism, where doing business is much more equal than it was four decades ago. Today, countries such as Malaysia, the United Arab Emirates, Thailand, Indonesia, Chile, and Panama—not to mention China and India—often can offer production conditions as good as, if not better than, those found in Europe, North America, Japan, and Oceania (table 5.2).

What about Revenue?

At a time when future deficits are at the top of the policy agenda, it seems odd to cut corporate taxes and sacrifice tax revenue, no matter what the long-term payoff in US jobs and living standards. Estimates published by the Joint

Table 5.2 Top-ranked non-OECD member countries on the Global Competitiveness Index, 2011–12

Country	Rank	Score
Hong Kong	11	4.58
Taiwan	13	5.26
Qatar	14	5.24
Saudi Arabia	17	5.17
Malaysia	21	5.08
China	26	4.90
United Arab Emirates	27	4.43
Brunei Darussalam	28	4.78
Oman	32	4.64
Kuwait	34	4.62
Bahrain	37	4.54
Thailand	39	4.52
Tunisia	40	4.47
Barbados	42	4.44
Lithuania	44	4.41
Indonesia	46	4.38
Cyprus	47	4.36
Panama	49	4.35
South Africa	50	4.34

OECD = Organization for Economic Cooperation and Development

Source: World Economic Forum, *Global Competitiveness Report 2011–2012*, www3.weforum.org/docs/WEF_GCR_Report_2011-12.pdf (accessed on March 25, 2013).

Committee on Taxation and used by the Congressional Budget Office (CBO) routinely project that cutting the corporate tax rate would reduce corporate tax receipts, if nothing else were changed (i.e., the static view).[4] In real life, other magnitudes do change when tax rates are lowered or raised. Such static estimates ignore the logic behind cutting the corporate tax rate in the first place: a positive boost to US business activity.

In light of this static bias in official estimates, it is worth reporting research that supports a dynamic view: namely, that cutting the corporate tax rate would

---

4. In the same static spirit, the Committee for a Responsible Federal Budget (2012) estimates that cutting the corporate tax rate to 25 percent would add $1 trillion to the federal debt through 2021.

reduce revenue much less than supposed by static estimates. For example, the Institute for Research on the Economics of Taxation (IRET) has constructed a model of the US economy to examine a variety of tax policy reforms. Using this model, IRET ran simulations to estimate the potential economic impact of a 10 percentage point cut in the corporate tax rate.[5] Cutting the corporate tax rate would prompt a jump of 6.3 percent in the private business capital stock, raise the average wage rate by 1.9 percent, and boost GDP by over 2 percent.[6] Federal receipts from corporate taxation would drop by $52 billion. On net, however, federal receipts would rise by $19 billion, or 0.8 percent, due to offsetting rises in personal income, Social Security, and Medicare taxes (see table 5.3 for results from the model).

Similarly, table 5.4 reports a panel regression of corporate tax revenues expressed as a percent of GDP in OECD countries. Table 5.5 breaks out corporate tax revenue from total tax revenue in select OECD countries as of 2008. In this exercise, tax revenues are regressed against the corporate statutory tax rate (federal, state, and local combined), controlling for country fixed effects. The very small though statistically significant coefficient—a negative value of 0.04—indicates that a 1 percentage point increase in the corporate tax rate may slightly decrease corporate tax revenue expressed as a percentage of GDP. In other words, there is a very small but negative connection between tax revenue and statutory tax rates within the range of rates implemented by OECD countries over the past quarter century—a range that covers statutory rates between roughly 20 and 40 percent.

Another empirical study by Karel Mertens and Morten O. Ravn (2011) supports the claim that cutting the corporate tax rate would not reduce revenues, indicating that the current corporate tax rate is positioned on the right-hand side of the Laffer curve.[7] Using US data from 1950 to 2006, Mertens and Ravn find the "increase in the tax base is sufficiently large that the corporate income tax cut leads to a small decline in corporate tax revenues only after the first quarter and a surplus thereafter." They conclude that "cuts in corporate income taxes are approximately self-financing." They further find that "a one percentage point cut in the [average effective corporate tax rate] raises real GDP per capita on impact by 0.5 percent and by 0.7 percent after five quarters."

Judging from their revenue estimates, neither the CBO nor the Office of Management and Budget subscribes to the research just cited. But many

---

5. These estimates are pegged off the CBO's 2008 baseline projections and assume a continuation of 100 percent bonus depreciation.

6. Stephen J. Entin and William McBride, "Simulating the Economic Effects of Romney's Tax Plan," Tax Foundation, www.taxfoundation.org/article/simulating-economic-effects-romneys-tax-plan (accessed on April 16, 2013).

7. Arthur Laffer (2004) makes much of the claim that after a certain level, high tax rates diminish tax revenue owing to evasion, avoidance, and a decrease in economic activity. Research by Mertens and Ravn (2011) did not support a Laffer curve effect for personal income taxes, but it did support the effect for US corporate taxes given the rates in effect over the period from 1950 to 2006.

Table 5.3 IRET model: Effects of a 10 percentage point cut in the corporate tax rate

Item	2008 level (billions of dollars) Baseline	Simulations	Change between baseline and simulation Billions of dollars	Percent
GDP	14,441	14,767	326	2.3
Private business output	10,728	10,979	251	2.3
Private business capital stock	27,608	29,357	1,749	6.3
Wage rate (dollars per hour)	33	34	1	1.9
Private business hours of work (billions of hours)	192	193	1	0.4
Federal tax receipts, of which:	2,503	2,522	19	0.8
Federal personal income taxes	1,102	1,146	43	3.9
Federal corporate profits tax (accruals)	181	129	−52	−28.7
Federal Social Security and Medicare receipts	974	997	22	2.3
State and local tax receipts, of which:	2,036	2,085	48	2.4
State and local personal income taxes	302	314	11	3.8
State and local corporate profits tax (accruals)	51	51	0	−0.1

Note: The baseline and simulation scenarios both assume continuation of the expensing rule in place since 2008 (50 percent bonus expensing).

Source: Institute for Research on the Economics of Taxation (IRET), 2010, www.iret.org.

members of Congress and independent economists do. So here's a suggestion: enact a corporate rate cut of 10 percentage points phased in at 2 percentage points a year, starting in 2013. If the revenue yield predicted by dynamic scoring (adjusted for the business cycle) fails to materialize, then postpone the next phase of the rate cut. To complement the cut, close a few genuine loopholes and take measures to arrest and even roll back the migration of large firms from the corporate tax system.

Whatever changes are made to the corporate tax system, it seems unlikely that corporate tax revenue will play a significant role in addressing the revenue side of a future compromise in addressing the problem of excessive public deficits and debt. Higher corporate rates will not raise much money because more corporations will transform themselves into pass-through entities and find other means of avoidance. Lower corporate tax rates will not lose much revenue, but neither will the dynamic effects be strong enough to raise much revenue. For significant new revenue, the United States should look to sources that are

Table 5.4 Corporate tax revenues regressed on the consolidated tax rate for OECD countries, 1981–2007

		Explanatory variables			
Dependent variable	Constant	Combined corporate tax rate	R-squared	Observations	Clusters
Corporate tax revenues/GDP	4.42*** (0.178)	−0.04*** (0.005)	0.04	640	29

OECD = Organization for Economic Cooperation and Development

Notes: Standard errors of the coefficient estimates are reported in parentheses. Estimation using the underlying panel dataset includes country fixed effects (not reported). *** denotes statistical significance at the 1 percent level. Clusters are the number of countries covered by the panel dataset.

Source: Hufbauer and DeRosa (2010).

less distortionary than corporate taxation. We recommend following the path of all other advanced countries by enacting a federal consumption tax.[8]

Grubert's Challenge

This chapter will later survey econometric findings that document the importance of corporate taxation as a factor affecting the location of production. But we start by reprising a recent econometric study that challenges conventional wisdom. Based on corporate tax return data for 754 large nonfinancial corporations (MNCs) from 1996 to 2004, Grubert (2012) reached two noteworthy findings. The first was that corporate tax differentials between the United States and foreign countries make little difference to the shares of production that take place at home or abroad, measured by the geographic origin of sales. Since Grubert did not have investment data, the production origin of sales stands as a proxy for the location of investment. Grubert's second noteworthy finding was that the location of pretax profit margins on sales responds sharply to tax differentials. Thus, the relative pretax profit margin on sales originating in the United States (a high-tax location) is much lower than the pretax profit margin on sales originating abroad (low-tax on average).

The starting point for Grubert's investigation was the expanding share of aggregate pretax worldwide income earned abroad by the 754 MNCs in his study. Their income rose from 37.1 percent in 1996 to 51.1 percent in 2004, a 14 percentage point shift in the share of worldwide income.[9]

---

8. For more details on what this type of tax would look like and why we consider it to be the best option, see Hufbauer and Vieiro (2012a).

9. In Grubert's calculation, domestic income earned by the MNCs was defined to exclude dividends received from foreign subsidiaries but to include interest and royalties received from foreign affiliates.

Table 5.5 Tax revenue for select OECD countries, 2008 (percent of GDP)

Country	Total tax revenue		Corporate tax revenue		VAT/GST revenue	
	Federal	State and local	Federal	State and local	Federal	State and local
Canada	14.0	15.4	2.2	1.2	1.9	0.8
Denmark	35.0	11.9	3.0	0.3	10.1	0.0
Finland	21.3	9.4	2.7	0.8	8.4	0.8
France	15.3	5.3	2.9	1.2	6.7	0.0
Germany	11.5	11.4	0.5	1.4	3.9	3.2
Italy	22.7	7.0	3.4	0.3	5.6	0.4
Japan	9.3	8.0	2.0	1.8	2.0	0.5
Korea	16.3	4.4	3.9	1.2	4.3	0.0
New Zealand	31.5	2.1	4.4	0.0	8.5	0.0
Norway	37.8	5.1	12.4	1.2	7.4	0.0
Spain	10.8	10.4	2.5	0.3	2.4	2.7
Sweden	24.6	16.1	3.0	1.2	9.3	0.0
Switzerland	10.8	11.6	1.6	1.7	3.7	0.0
Turkey	16.1	2.1	1.6	0.2	4.4	0.6
United Kingdom	27.0	1.7	3.6	0.0	6.4	0.0
United States	10.4	9.4	1.6	0.3	...	0.0
OECD total	21.0	8.4	3.2	0.0	6.5	1.0

OECD = Organization for Economic Cooperation and Development; VAT = value-added tax; GST = goods and services tax

Source: OECD Revenue Statistics, 1965–2009.

Grubert found that the declining percentage of worldwide income reported in the United States largely reflects a decline in the profit margin earned on US sales and a corresponding rise in the profit margin on foreign sales—not, he stresses, a change in the national location of production.[10]

Among US tax law features that facilitate the decline of reported profits on US sales, Grubert highlighted the difficulty of ascertaining market prices for intellectual property transferred from parent MNCs to their foreign subsidiaries and the "check the box" feature that enables parent MNCs to characterize a foreign subsidiary as a branch for US tax law purposes even though foreign tax authorities characterize the same subsidiary as a separate corporate entity.

In 1996, the average foreign effective tax rate for Grubert's corporate sample

---

10. For the purpose of defining production origin, US exports are included in US sales while US imports are included in foreign sales. The core statistical analysis was carried out for 415 MNCs that had positive profits both in 1996 and 2004.

was 21.3 percent.[11] This is the rate on foreign earnings and profits, a corporate income concept approximating US taxable income. The effective US rate on repatriated earnings was the US statutory corporate rate, namely 35 percent.[12] In 2004, the average foreign effective rate had declined to 15.9 percent, while the effective US rate on repatriated earnings was still 35 percent. In other words, the differential between the US tax on repatriated earnings and the foreign tax on earnings not repatriated widened from 13.7 to 19.1 percentage points.

Grubert's statistical analysis indicated that a 10 percentage point increase in the differential between US and foreign tax rates prompts a 9 percentage point rise in the average foreign profit margin on sales and a 7.5 percentage point fall in the average US profit margin. This finding led him to argue that the initial 1996 tax differential (13.7 percentage points) plus the widening between 1996 and 2004 (another 5.4 percentage points) were together responsible for 12 percentage points of the 14 percentage shift in worldwide corporate income from domestic to foreign sources. Most of the shift occurred because US tax law is flexible as to the location (domestic or foreign "source") of income arising from intangible property—trade secrets, trade names, patents, and copyrights. Given this flexibility, MNCs take steps to ensure that intangible property income is largely earned in low tax jurisdictions abroad.

According to JPMorgan (2012), the stock of earnings held by affiliates abroad rose from $1.4 trillion in 2010 to $1.7 trillion in 2012, a gain of about $150 billion per year. Grubert's calculations indicate a 19 percentage point differential between the average foreign tax rate on affiliate earnings (around 16 percent) and the US statutory rate (35 percent). Hence a purely static revenue calculation—a calculation that assumes nothing changes in the real world when firms are subjected to higher taxes—indicates that applying the US statutory rate to unrepatriated foreign earnings would bring $29 billion annually to the US Treasury.[13] Such calculations assume that US production and sales would chug right along as if nothing had happened. MNCs, whether headquartered in the United States or abroad, would continue to view the United States as a fine investment and production location, despite the gap of 19 percentage points in US and foreign effective tax rates.

---

11. The average effective foreign tax rate for each MNC is calculated by combining taxes paid and income earned in all the foreign countries where the MNC does business.

12. As a general rule, foreign source income is taxed at the US statutory rate, less the applicable foreign tax credit. Since the foreign tax credit corresponds to foreign taxes paid, the combined effective US-plus-foreign tax rate is 35 percent on foreign income when remitted to the United States. However, remitted foreign income usually brings with it a foreign tax credit above 30 percent, so the additional tax paid to the US Treasury is ordinarily less than 5 percent.

13. Some static calculations reach even more extravagant results based on the assumption that applying the US statutory rate worldwide would eliminate income shifting and thus avoid foreign taxation (and the foreign tax credit) on a very large chunk of corporate earnings. Kimberly Clausing (2009), for example, asserts that income shifting deprived the US Treasury of somewhere between $57 billion and $90 billion in revenue in 2008. Like other static estimates, this takes no account of production, jobs, and tax revenue that would be lost if the high US statutory rate were applied to the worldwide operations of US MNCs.

Reality Check

Few observers believe that the United States could impose corporate taxes at an effective rate 19 percentage points higher than the average of its foreign competitors without adversely affecting investment, production, and employment decisions. The high and rising mobility of economic activity argues otherwise (appendix B).

What does the econometric evidence say about taxes and investment? Fortunately for our purposes, Ruud A. de Mooij and Sjef Ederveen (2008) surveyed and distilled a vast body of econometric analysis. To do this, they created a "meta sample" of 427 observations. Each observation is an independent study that estimated the impact of corporate tax—measured in different ways (statutory tax rates, effective marginal tax rates, approximate average tax rate, etc.)—on investment decisions and the tax base.

Combining these studies allowed the authors to formulate a "consensus estimate" of –3.1 for the semi-tax elasticity of the tax base.[14] The semi-tax elasticity measures the percent change in the corporate tax base for each one percentage point change in the tax rate. The consensus estimate says that a one percentage point increase in the tax rate results in a 3.1 percent decline in the tax base. The authors break this impact into five "decision margins" (channels that managers use in making decisions): organization form, financial policy, profit-shifting, investment-intensive, and investment-extensive.[15] The respective semi-elasticities are –0.70, –0.15, –1.20, –0.40, and –0.65.

Each decision margin represents choices made by companies in determining where and how to invest. For example, organization form reflects a company's decision in terms of incorporation, branch, partnership, or other business structure. Higher corporate taxes discourage firms from incorporating; instead they opt for other business forms, especially pass-through entities. The meta-analysis suggests that an increase in the corporate tax rate by one percentage point decreases the corporate tax base on average by 0.7 percent via a shift from corporate organization to pass-through-entity organization. The adverse impact on the tax base of an increase in the corporate tax rate is even larger through the investment channel: A one percentage point increase in the tax rate leads to a 1.05 percent decrease in the tax base through lower investment, combining the intensive and extensive semi-elasticity values.

Since many of the studies collected in meta-analysis are dated, and since economic activity is increasingly mobile (again, see appendix B), it seems likely that the adverse investment impact of higher taxation is greater now than the reported combined semi-elasticity of –1.05.

---

14. The authors regressed a vector of all the estimation elasticities on several dummy variables to control for differences between studies such as data characteristics (e.g., type of capital and time), the tax variable, and background characteristics (e.g., method of double-tax relief and source of financing). In the view of the authors, the resulting semi-elasticity values cited above are additive.

15. Intensive investments are typically in assets entailing fewer risks and lower returns. Extensive investments refer to assets that are riskier and offer higher returns.

In the Mooij and Ederveen dissection of decision margins, profit shifting (another name for income shifting) shows the largest semi-elasticity: A one percentage point increase in the corporate tax rate decreases the tax base by 1.2 percent. This finding accords with Grubert's subsequent research. However, from its meta-analysis, the OECD (2008, 62) concluded "that the share of FDI that comprises real investment in physical capital is more responsive to taxes than other components of FDI."

Reconciling the Research

As Mooij and Ederveen (2008) report, multiple studies conducted over the past two decades conclude that corporate tax rates make a difference to investment and production location. But Grubert reports that effective tax differences between the United States and the foreign average have little impact on production in the United States (measured by sales) and, by inference, investment in the United States. Can these findings be reconciled?

Yes. But reconciliation requires a completely different mindset than the views expressed by, among others, President Obama.[16] Flexibility in US tax law is not about using tax breaks to ship jobs overseas. Quite the contrary. Flexibility enables the United States to stay in the game. It enables MNCs (whether headquartered in the United States or abroad) to pay competitive effective rates on their worldwide income, even while producing a substantial quantity of goods and services in the United States. Accordingly, the US jobs and production picture is not nearly so bad as it would be if US MNC activity worldwide were taxed at the high US statutory rate. More US production and jobs, despite an oppressive statutory corporate tax rate, are better national outcomes than extracting a bigger tax bite from US corporate income. If tax flexibility did not exist, a likely counterfactual scenario would find mobile production of goods and services shipped overseas to a far larger extent.

It is also important to note that the Grubert study deals only with the share of total MNC income earned at home and abroad and not with the overall level of that income. Given the numerous studies that have documented the high level of responsiveness of firm production to corporate tax rates, we would expect there to be aggregate effects that are not picked up by Grubert's measures. Thus, while raising the tax rate on US MNC activity to a universally high level everywhere in the world might not have a tremendous impact on where firms produce, it will most likely have a negative impact on how much they produce, both at home and abroad.

These facts should guide policy officials. Reducing the US corporate tax rate is certainly the most efficient way to encourage domestic investment and associated gains in production and jobs. Doing so would boost outward FDI as domestic firms would invest more domestically and abroad (see again table

16. For the extensive record of Obama's views on the taxation of MNCs, see Hufbauer and Vieiro (2011) and Hufbauer and Wong (2011). See also footnote 1 in chapter 1.

5.3)—a counterintuitive outcome to those who think in terms of substitution rather than complementarity. Raising the effective tax rate that US MNCs pay on their foreign operations should not be viewed as an alternative approach with similar ends. Higher taxes on foreign operations will not encourage US MNCs to invest domestically. Instead, they will encourage US MNCs to slow their global expansion (and hence their US expansion). And they will encourage some US MNCs to reincorporate the parent company abroad. In fact, at least 10 public companies have done so since 2009, citing the high US statutory tax rate as a primary motivation.[17] Much of the anti-MNC rhetoric is inspired by the supposed "hollowing out" of the US labor force and the decline in domestic manufacturing employment. However, if President Obama's policies are enacted, politicians will soon be complaining that not only jobs are being shipped overseas but also corporate headquarters.

Some scholars cite the aftermath of the Homeland Investment Act of 2004 (HIA) as an argument against any form of territorial tax system. The HIA, which was an important component of the American Jobs Creation Act of 2004, gave US MNCs a one-year holiday in 2005 to repatriate earnings from their foreign subsidiaries at the reduced US tax rate of 5.25 percent. Congressional advocates of the HIA claimed that a burst of US investment and job creation would follow. There was indeed a burst of repatriations in 2005 by about $200 billion over the normal annual level of about $100 billion. In a retrospective analysis, however, Dhammika Dharmapala, C. Fritz Foley, and Kristin J. Forbes (2011) found little new investment or job creation by the parent corporations. Instead, shareholder payouts increased by 60 to 92 cents for each $1 increase in repatriated earnings.[18] This outcome is consistent with the assumption that MNCs were not financially constrained in the mid-2000s, just as they are not financially constrained today. To be sure, higher shareholder payouts and an associated increase in share values are both good for the US economy,[19] but that is not the central reason for advocating a permanent territorial system, as opposed to a temporary holiday. A permanent system will create a level playing field for US MNCs in head-to-head competition abroad with MNCs based in practically all other countries. At the same time, a permanent territorial system will help the United States maintain its attraction as a headquarters country for MNCs.

---

17. See John D. McKinnon and Scott Thurm, "U.S. Firms Move Abroad to Cut Taxes," *Wall Street Journal*, August 28, 2012, http://online.wsj.com/article_email/SB1000087239639044423050457 76152-32602107536-lMyQjAxMTAyMDIwOTAyODk3Wj.html?mod=wsj_valetbottom_email (accessed on March 25, 2013).

18. Michael Faulkender and Mitchell Petersen (2009) examined a subset of financially constrained firms and found that they did increase domestic investment but not employment. Other authors cited by Dharmapala, Foley, and Forbes (2011) found no overall effect of the HIA on capital expenditures.

19. As Dharmapala, Foley, and Forbes (2011) note, shareholder payouts inspire both investment and consumption. Mitchell Oler, Terry Shevlin, and Ryan Wilson (2007) found that share values increased in the run-up to the HIA for firms with earnings in low-tax jurisdictions.

6

Implications for US Policy

The evidence presented in this study shows that US-headquartered multinational corporations are the most productive and highest-paying segment of the US economy. They conduct more R&D, provide more value added to US domestic inputs, and export more goods and services than other firms in the American economy. The superior technology and management techniques they employ spill over in both horizontal and vertical directions to improve the performance of local firms and workers. Their corporate social responsibility activities provide tangible benefits to the communities where they locate their plants and research facilities. Perhaps most important in the context of the contemporary backlash against globalization is our finding that outward foreign direct investment (FDI) is not a substitute but rather a complement to the positive features of the American economy in the form of better jobs, larger investment, greater exports, and more R&D. US policymakers can expect that measures taken to impede or retard US MNC expansion abroad will weaken job creation, investment, R&D, and exports at home, rather than strengthening or enhancing domestic economic activity.

In an era when the United States wants not just to expand employment but also to create well-paying jobs that will reverse the declining earnings of many American workers and middle-class families, it is more important than ever to enhance the United States as an attractive business location for US and foreign multinationals. We should want these firms to locate their most dynamic and productive operations in the United States.

Tax Reform First

Our recommendation is clear: For its own prosperity, the United States badly needs to reform its corporate tax system, especially with respect to earnings at home. As the Simpson-Bowles Commission and others have urged, the federal corporate rate should be cut to 25 percent or lower (Hufbauer and Wong 2011). Within this range, the rate cut will be approximately self-financing, as firms will have less resort to pass-through entities, undertake more investment, and engage in less profit-shifting.

For earnings abroad, dividends paid by foreign corporate subsidiaries to their US parent firm should be taxed at a reduced rate. We do not delve into details here, but the Joint Committee on Taxation (2011) has summarized the territorial tax systems of major countries, while Harry G. Grubert and Rosanne Altshuler (2012), among others, have offered a proposal for US reform. Above all, Congress should refuse to enact faux "reforms" that would impose the current high US statutory tax rate on the worldwide income of US MNCs. Instead, Congress should enact genuine reforms that reduce the US corporate tax rate and embrace a permanent territorial system for taxing overseas earnings. This combination will reduce the incentive for tax arbitrage as the US tax system more closely conforms to world norms.

A simpler and better corporate tax law could deliver substantial benefits to the US economy. The good news is that corporate tax reform need not mean a loss of tax revenue (Hufbauer and Vieiro 2012b). Lower rates will automatically enlarge the corporate tax base, as firms will be less frantic in their search for tax shelters and as US production rises. (This is the positive side of the income-shifting phenomenon.) With a territorial system, the US competitive position in world markets would be enhanced. Moreover US-based MNCs could then repatriate a significant part of the $1.7 trillion stock of earnings held abroad for distribution to shareholders or productive investment in the United States without incurring a substantial US tax burden.[1] Over the long haul, US-based MNCs could compete with foreign-based MNCs on equivalent tax terms in third-country markets. Faster expansion by US MNCs abroad, abetted by a territorial tax system, would bring many benefits to the US economy. Americans should welcome, not fear, outward investment by US MNCs. This is the essence of complementarity analysis.

At the same time, the United States should undertake policy initiatives to enhance its own attraction as a place to do business. US prosperity will not be advanced by restricting investment abroad, but it can be advanced by reforms at home, as described below.

---

1. As mentioned earlier, JPMorgan (2012) estimates the stock of earnings held abroad at $1.7 trillion, up from $1.4 trillion in 2010. The arguments that a territorial system would lead to substantial repatriation of foreign earnings (up to $1 trillion) are set forth by Laura Tyson, Kenneth Serwin, and Eric Drabkin (2011). Based on the experience of the 2004 Homeland Investment Act, it is an open question what portion might be distributed to shareholders as dividends or share buybacks and what portion might be invested in R&D or plant and equipment. Following the 2004 act, the bulk of repatriated earnings (60 to 90 percent) were used to finance shareholder payouts, in a period—much like today—when MNCs were not financially constrained. However, a complementary sharp cut in the US corporate tax rate would shift business decisions toward higher investments rather than a surge in shareholder payouts.

Much Better Education

US-based and foreign multinationals target the United States for investment overwhelmingly because the American economy gives them access to skilled and energetic workers. The US workforce today is more willing to work long hours, often at multiple jobs, than workers in other advanced countries. However, after more than a century of spectacular progress, the rate of US educational advancement has sharply decelerated in recent years. From 1940 to 1980, the mean educational attainment of all US workers climbed by 0.86 years per decade (from 9.01 years to 12.46 years), but from 1980 to 2005 the total increase was no more than one year—only 0.43 years per decade.[2]

This slowdown in US educational progress has taken place while improvements in secondary education have been accelerating around the world. Other countries have not merely been catching up to the US workforce, they have been moving ahead. Among 26 OECD member countries in 2006, 18 had high school graduation rates higher than the United States.

At the same time, the quality of US education is a matter of severe concern, with US students scoring below the median in comparative tests of educational achievement in science and mathematics. Maintaining the competitive quality of the US labor force is a dynamic process. As Jacob Kirkegaard (2007) points out, the retirement of the "baby boomer" generation in the United States represents the largest brain drain (or skill drain) that has ever taken place in any economy in history, and replacement indicators are not promising. Measures to improve the education and skill level of the American workforce are therefore vital to make the United States an attractive site for international investment.

Immigration Reform

A particularly important component of improving human capital resources within the US labor market is the policy regarding high-skilled immigration. Immigrants with college or higher degrees bring skills directly into the US labor pool, innovative ideas for new goods and services, and connections to business networks in their home countries. Approximately a quarter of all US high-tech startups since the early 1990s have had at least one foreign-born cofounder, up from less than 10 percent in the 1970s (Kirkegaard 2007). Yet the US H1-B visa program for foreign workers now places stringent caps on the inflow of engineers, scientists, architects, doctors, and managers from abroad.

As recently as the 1990s, the quota caps on H1-B visas were rarely reached, and even in 2003 the cap was still at 195,000 skilled workers annually. But Congress has progressively reduced the cap and, as a result, the most competitive companies in the United States—including US affiliates of foreign MNCs—cannot get visas for the non-US high-skilled workers they need to hire. In 2008, about half of 163,000 US companies wishing to hire foreign high-skilled

---

2. See Kirkegaard (2007), Goldin and Katz (2008), and Baily and Slaughter (2008).

workers on H-1B visas were denied this opportunity because of the annual quota of 85,000 permits then available (Kirkegaard 2008). The quota cap has since been slashed to 65,000 workers annually. Any US firm that wanted to hire a foreign-born high-skilled worker in December 2011 had to wait until April 1, 2012, as the FY2012 quota had already been filled.[3] Unfortunately, Congress also takes a dim view of immigration provisions in US free trade agreements: Since the Chilean and Singapore agreements, which were ratified in 2002, no US free trade agreement has contained an immigration chapter (Stephenson and Hufbauer 2011).

There is, however, a ray of sunshine in US visa policy: L visas are available for intracorporate transfers of managers (L-1 visas) and skilled employees (L-2 visas), and about 75,000 of these were issued in 2010. Unfortunately, the eligibility requirements for L visas mean that they are not available for new hires. Liberalization of US policy (essentially H-1B visas) toward new high-skilled immigrants would make the American economy more competitive as a site for US and non-US investors alike.

World-Class Infrastructure

State-of-the-art infrastructure—ports, airports, railroads, roads, bridges, tunnels, information technology, and electrical grids—is crucial to enable MNCs to manage worldwide production and coordinate international supply chains. While alternative host-country sites around the world are upgrading their infrastructure in clearly visible ways, the United States is falling behind in both relative and absolute terms. US spending on public infrastructure has been declining on both a gross and net basis. The American Society of Civil Engineers awarded a grade of "D" to the quality of US infrastructure in its *2009 Report Card for America's Infrastructure*.[4] In grading 15 segments of US infrastructure ranging from aviation to roads, bridges, transmission lines, and wastewater, the report cited delayed maintenance and chronic underfunding as contributors to poor outcomes.

Countries such as Singapore have demonstrated that high-quality infrastructure delivers high social returns. Despite such evidence, however, two critical obstacles limit investment in infrastructure in the United States. First, most US infrastructure is publicly financed, and public budgets are depleted at the federal and state level by Medicare, Medicaid, Social Security, state pensions, and defense needs. Second, most rights-of-way for everything from airports to ports, roads, and transmission lines are either in the public domain

---

3. "USCIS Reaches Fiscal Year 2012 H-1B Cap," US Citizenship and Immigration Services press release, November 23, 2011, www.uscis.gov/portal/site/uscis/menuitem.5af9bb95919f35e66f614 176543f6d1a/?vgnextoid=f0a78614e90d3310VgnVCM100000082ca60aRCRD&vgnextchannel=6 8439c7755cb9010VgnVCM10000045f3d6a1RCRD (accessed on March 25, 2013).

4. American Society of Civil Engineers, *2009 Report Card for America's Infrastructure*, www.infrastructurereportcard.org/2009/report-cards (accessed on March 25, 2013).

or severely regulated by public agencies. The pathway to adequate finance is the adoption of user-pay (toll) systems on a grand scale for virtually all forms of infrastructure, applying the latest technology (e.g., EZ Pass and credit cards) for collecting fees from the public. The pathway to engaging private firms is through long-term leases of public rights-of-way and speedier processes for creating rights-of-way for new infrastructure (e.g., transmission lines from wind farms to cities).

Conclusion

This study has shown that as US MNCs expand their global operations, they become more productive, expand output, provide more high-wage and high-benefit jobs, and undertake more R&D at home as well as abroad. Beyond creating a hospitable framework for outward investment, it is distinctly in the interest of the United States to create a policy environment that encourages US MNCs to use the domestic economy as the central point of their international operations. The United States could dramatically enhance its attraction as a magnet for MNCs and as a base of production for global markets. Policies to this end are readily available. To enhance investment, production, and job creation at home, corporate tax reform, better education, liberalized immigration, and world-class infrastructure are all essential. To enlarge the global footprint of US MNCs, and spur associated production, jobs, and R&D in America, territorial taxation is the answer. Political leaders in both parties frequently promise to improve life for middle-class Americans. These policies would be a good place to start. With wrong choices, the same policy areas could also be major ingredients for failure.

Appendices

Appendix A

Table A.1   Regression result details for figures 3.1 and 4.2

Model	1	2	3	4	5
Number of observations	46,438	46,566	22,646	11,470	44,255
Dependent variable	Δln par emp	Δln par sales	Δln par ex	Δln par R&D	Δln par capx
Δln affiliate emp	0.394***	0.414***	0.423***	0.536***	0.427***
	(0.012)	(0.012)	(0.026)	(0.049)	(0.016)
Fixed year effects	yes	yes	yes	yes	yes
R-squared	0.18	0.16	0.08	0.04	0.07
Model	**6**	**7**	**8**	**9**	**10**
Number of observations	45,982	46,201	22,083	11,483	43,723
Dependent variable	Δln par emp	Δln par sales	Δln par ex	Δln par R&D	Δln par capx
Δln affiliate sales	0.227***	0.258***	0.332***	0.704***	0.249***
	(0.010)	(0.011)	(0.024)	(0.044)	(0.013)
Fixed year effects	yes	yes	yes	yes	yes
R-squared	0.1	0.11	0.07	0.06	0.04
Model	**11**	**12**	**13**	**14**	**15**
Number of observations	11,392	11,380	7,612	6,897	10,423
Dependent variable	Δln par emp	Δln par sales	Δln par ex	Δln par R&D	Δln par capx
Δln affiliate R&D	0.061***	0.062***	0.080***	0.239***	0.116***
	(0.006)	(0.006)	(0.013)	(0.043)	(0.039)
Fixed year effects	yes	yes	yes	yes	yes
R-squared	0.02	0.01	0.01	0.02	0.02

(continues on next page)

Table A.1 Regression result details for figures 3.1 and 4.2 *(continued)*

Model	16	17	18	19	20
Number of observations	30,247	30,351	14,597	8,854	28,815
Dependent variable	Δln par emp	Δln par sales	Δln par ex	Δln par R&D	Δln par capx
Δln affiliate capx	0.087***	0.095***	0.108***	0.159***	0.132***
	(0.005)	(0.005)	(0.011)	(0.019)	(0.008)
Fixed year effects	yes	yes	yes	yes	yes
R-squared	0.04	0.03	0.02	0.02	0.03

Notes: Δ indicates year-over-year change and "ln" denotes the natural logarithm. "par" refers to the domestic operations of the parent firm and "affiliate" denotes foreign operations. The variables of interest are employment (emp), sales, exports (ex), R&D, and capital expenditures (capx). *** indicates statistical significance at the 1 percent level. Standard errors appear in parentheses.

Source: Authors' calculations.

Appendix B
Mobility of US Private Economic Activity

Not long ago, virtually all banking services required a visit to the local bank. Now, telebanking and websites allow banking customers to conduct many of these transactions from any location. In other words, banking has become much more mobile. Technology is continually increasing the range of goods and services that are mobile, in the sense that sellers and buyers can do business at a distance.

While international trade data provide a barometer of which goods and services are currently mobile, they understate the true degree of mobility if we lived in a "frictionless" world (meaning no tariffs or nontariff barriers and no border obstacles). Moreover, data on services trade are notoriously poor. To address these measurement problems, J. Bradford Jensen (2011) pioneered an ingenious method for estimating the extent to which US services are mobile. Applying Jensen's approach, we estimate that 66 percent of US production of goods is mobile and 72 percent of US production of services is mobile. Taken together, 69 percent of private GDP is mobile (table B.1) and 46 percent of private-sector employment is mobile (table B.2). The sections below outline Jensen's method as well as our extension of it.

Jensen's Original Approach

Jensen and Lori Kletzer (2005) developed an empirical approach to identify tradable services activity, described as "tradability." Later, Jensen (2011) applied the approach to a wide range of services industries and occupations. We equate "tradability" with "mobility." The concept of tradability is based on the mismatch between the location of production and the location of consumption within the United States. For example, there is a close correspondence between the geographic location of the population and the number of barber shops and beauty salons. These services are difficult to deliver at a distance—they are classic nontradable services. In contrast, there are significant concentrations of software production in the Seattle metropolitan area and in Silicon Valley. Most of the software produced in these regions is not consumed locally but is instead sold to users in other regions.

When production is concentrated at a distance from consumption, Jensen infers that the output of services production is traded within the United States. Using tradability within the United States as an indicator of international trade potential, we can identify at a detailed level which services activities "ought" to be traded internationally.

Jensen finds that many services—movie and music recording production, software production, R&D services, and engineering services, to cite a few examples—appear to be "traded" (that is, transacted across distances) within the United States and thus are potentially tradable across international borders.

Jensen applies his methodology to calculate a locational Gini coefficient for each North American Industry Classification System (NAICS) code. The coefficient measures the degree of dispersion between production and consumption across the United States. A locational Gini coefficient of 1.0 would indicate that production and consumption of that good or service is totally "traded" across the United States. A locational Gini coefficient of 0.0 would indicate that the service is produced and consumed in the same geographic location.

Based on a qualitative assessment of industry activity, Jensen considers that an activity is "tradable" when its locational Gini coefficient exceeds 0.1. For example, this threshold characterizes retail trade services (such as supermarkets, clothing stores, etc.) as nontradable. It classifies transportation services as tradable. We adopt Jensen's threshold for our analysis.

Extension of the Jensen-Kletzer (2005) Approach

While Jensen and Kletzer limited their focus to services, they calculated locational Gini coefficients for all NAICS codes covering both goods and services. For our purposes, we gathered data on US GDP and employment for each two-digit NAICS code. Since the locational Gini coefficients of Jensen and Kletzer refer to the disaggregated four-digit level, we calculated the average locational Gini coefficient for each two-digit NAICS code by weighting the four-digit coefficients by employment in each four-digit sector. These averages are reported in tables B.1 and B.2. By this measure, government services score as "tradable," but for international commerce that designation conflicts with political feasibility. Hence, our estimates are limited to "private GDP," excluding government spending. Similarly, public-sector employment is listed but excluded from the estimate as well. We then calculate the share of private GDP and employment that is tradable or mobile. The results make intuitive sense. Construction and utilities, for example, are not mobile, but information technology and management services are.

Table B.1 Mobility estimates of US production of goods and services

Industry	NAICS code	Average locational Gini coefficient	Tradable (yes/no)[a]	Product	Value added to US GDP (billions of dollars)	Share of private GDP (percent)[b]
Agriculture, forestry, fishing, and hunting	11	0.29	Y	Goods	156.90	1.2
Mining	21	0.51	Y	Goods	239.50	1.9
Utilities	22	0.05	N	Goods	264.80	2.1
Construction	23	0.08	N	Goods	511.60	4.1
Manufacturing	31–33	0.26	Y	Goods	1,701.90	13.6
Wholesale trade	42	0.14	Y	Goods	797.30	6.3
Retail trade	44–45	0.07	N	Goods	884.80	7.0
Transportation and warehousing	48–49	0.15	Y	Goods	402.50	3.2
Information	51	0.19	Y	Services	623.40	5.0
Finance and insurance	52	0.15	Y	Services	1,241.90	9.9
Real estate and rental and leasing	53	0.13	Y	Services	1,765.20	14.0
Professional, scientific, and technical services	54	0.19	Y	Services	1,095.70	8.7
Management of companies and enterprises	55	0.23	Y	Services	263.60	2.1
Administrative and waste management services	56	0.10	N	Services	423.30	3.4
Educational services	61	0.01	N	Services	163.10	1.3
Health care and social assistance	62	0.02	N	Services	1,109.10	8.8
Arts, entertainment, and recreation	71	0.12	Y	Services	139.10	1.1
Accommodation and food services	72	0.04	N	Services	416.60	2.2
Other services, except government	81	0.14	Y	Services	356.70	2.8
Government	92	0.16	N	Services	1,968.50	15.7

(continues on next page)

Table B.1   Mobility estimates of US production of goods and services *(continued)*

Industry	Value added to US GDP (billions of dollars)	Share of private GDP (percent)[b]
Subtotal of tradable private GDP in goods	3,298.10	26.2
Subtotal of private GDP in goods	4,959.30	39.4
Subtotal of tradable private GDP in services	5,485.60	43.6
Subtotal of private GDP in services	7,597.70	60.5
Total of tradable private GDP	8,783.70	69.9
Total private GDP	12,557.00	100.0

NAICS = North American Industry Classification System

a. Industry is considered "tradable" when the Gini coefficient is greater than 0.1.
b. Private GDP excludes government spending.

Sources: Bureau of Economic Analysis, www.bea.gov (for US GDP); Jensen (2011) (for locational Gini coefficient); and authors' calculations.

Table B.2   Mobility estimates of US employment

Industry	NAICS code	Average locational Gini coefficient	Tradable (yes/no)[a]	Product	Employment (in thousands)	Share of private-sector employment (percent)[b]
Agriculture, forestry, fishing, and hunting	11	0.29	Y	Goods	1,271	1.1
Mining	21	0.51	Y	Goods	648	0.5
Utilities	22	0.05	N	Goods	553	0.5
Construction	23	0.08	N	Goods	5,767	5.1
Manufacturing	31–33	0.26	Y	Goods	11,529	10.3
Wholesale trade	42	0.14	Y	Goods	5,520	4.9
Retail trade	44–45	0.07	N	Goods	14,743	13.2
Transportation and warehousing	48–49	0.15	Y	Goods	4,227	3.8
Information	51	0.19	Y	Services	2,720	2.4
Finance and insurance	52	0.15	Y	Services	5,720	5.1
Real estate and rental and leasing	53	0.13	Y	Services	2,015	1.8
Professional, scientific, and technical services	54	0.19	Y	Services	7,603	6.8
Management of companies and enterprises	55	0.23	Y	Services	1,853	1.6
Administrative and waste management services	56	0.10	N	Services	7,515	6.7
Educational services	61	0.01	N	Services	3,211	2.8
Health care and social assistance	62	0.02	N	Services	16,534	14.8
Arts, entertainment, and recreation	71	0.12	Y	Services	1,944	1.7
Accommodation and food services	72	0.04	N	Services	11,262	10.1
Other services, except government	81	0.14	Y	Services	6,743	6.0
Government	92	0.16	N	Services	24,966	n.a.

(continues on next page)

Table B.2   Mobility estimates of US employment *(continued)*

Industry	Employment (in thousands)	Share of private-sector employment (percent)[b]
Subtotal of tradable private-sector employment in goods	23,195.00	20.8
Subtotal of private-sector employment in goods	44,258.00	39.7
Subtotal of tradable private-sector employment in services	28,598.00	25.6
Subtotal of private-sector employment in services	67,120.00	60.2
Total of tradable private-sector employment	51,793.00	46.5
Total private-sector employment	111,378.00	0.8

n.a. = not available
NAICS = North American Industry Classification System

a. Industry is considered "tradable" when the Gini coefficient is greater than 0.1.
b. Private-sector employment excludes public-sector employees.

Sources: Bureau of Economic Analysis, www.bea.gov (for employment); Jensen (2011) (for locational Gini coefficient); and authors' calculations.

References

Amiti, Mary, and Katharine Wakelin. 2002. Investment Liberalization and International Trade. *Journal of International Economics* 61, no. 1: 101–26.

Antras, Pol, Luis Garicano, and Esteban Rossi-Hansberg. 2006. Offshoring in a Knowledge Economy. *Quarterly Journal of Economics* 121, no. 1: 31–77.

Auerbach, Alan J. 2006. *Why Have Corporate Tax Revenues Declined? Another Look.* NBER Working Paper 12463. Cambridge, MA: National Bureau of Economic Research.

Autor, David H., David Dorn, and Gordon H. Hanson. 2012. *The China Syndrome: Local Labor Market Effects of Import Competition in the United States.* NBER Working Paper 18054. Cambridge, MA: National Bureau of Economic Research.

Baily, Martin N., and Matthew J. Slaughter. 2008. *Strengthening US Competitiveness in the Global Economy.* Private Equity Council (December). Available at www.pegcc.org/wordpress/wp-content/uploads/pec_wp_strengthening_120908a.pdf (accessed on March 25, 2012).

Baldwin, Richard, and Frédéric Robert-Nicoud. 2010. *Trade-in-goods and Trade-in-tasks: An Integrating Framework.* NBER Working Paper 15882. Cambridge, MA: National Bureau of Economic Research.

Barefoot, Kevin B., and Raymond J. Mataloni, Jr. 2009. US Multinational Companies: Operations in the United States and Abroad in 2007. *Survey of Current Business* 89 (August): 63–87.

Barefoot, Kevin B., and Raymond J. Mataloni, Jr. 2011. Operations of US Multinational Companies in the United States and Abroad. Preliminary Results from the 2009 Benchmark Survey. *Survey of Current Business* 91, no. 11 (November): 29–48.

Bergsten, C. Fred, Thomas Horst, and Theodore H. Moran. 1978. *American Multinationals and American Interests.* Washington: Brookings Institution.

Bernard, Andrew B., J. Bradford Jensen, and Peter K. Schott. 2009. Importers, Exporters and Multinationals: A Portrait of Firms in the US that Trade Goods. In *Producer Dynamics: New Evidence from Micro Data,* ed. J. B. Jensen, T. Dunne, and M. Roberts. Chicago: University of Chicago Press for the National Bureau of Economic Research.

Blomström, Magnus, Robert E. Lipsey, and Ksenia Kulchyck. 1988. US and Swedish Direct Investment and Exports. In *Trade Policy Issues and Empirical Analysis,* ed. Robert E. Baldwin. Chicago: University of Chicago Press for the National Bureau of Economic Research.

Borga, Maria, and Robert E. Lipsey. 2009. Factor Prices, Factor Substitution and Exporting in US Manufacturing Affiliates Abroad. *World Economy* 32, no. 1: 30–48.

Brainard, S. Lael, and David A. Riker. 1997. *Are US Multinationals Exporting US Jobs?* NBER Working Paper 5958. Cambridge, MA: National Bureau of Economic Research.

Branstetter, Lee, and C. Fritz Foley. 2010. Facts and Fallacies about US FDI in China (with apologies to Rob Feenstra). In *China's Growing Role in World Trade,* ed. Robert C. Feenstra and Shang-Jin Wei. Chicago: University of Chicago Press for the National Bureau of Economic Research.

Chen, Duanjie, and Jack Mintz. 2012. Corporate Tax Competitiveness Rankings for 2012. *Cato Institute Tax and Budget Bulletin* 65 (September). Washington: Cato Institute.

Clausing, Kimberly A. 2009. Multinational Firm Tax Avoidance and Tax Policy. *National Tax Journal* 62, no. 4: 703–25.

Clausing, Kimberly A. 2012a. A Challenging Time for International Tax Policy. *Tax Notes* (July 16): 281–83.

Clausing, Kimberly A. 2012b. Response to Hufbauer: Territorial System Has Risks. *Tax Notes* (August 13): 825.

Cline, William R. 2010. Estimating the Impact of the Exchange Rate on the Trade Balance and Jobs. *Real Time Economic Issues Watch* (November 1). Washington: Peterson Institute for International Economics. Available at www.piie.com/blogs/realtime/?p=1806.

Committee for a Responsible Federal Budget. 2012. *Reforming the Corporate Tax Code.* Tax Working Paper Series. Washington.

Desai, Mihir. 2009. *Securing Jobs or the New Protectionism? Taxing the Overseas Activities of Multinational Firms.* Harvard Business School Finance Working Paper 09-107. Boston, MA: Harvard Business School.

Desai, Mihir A., C. Fritz Foley, and James R. Hines, Jr. 2005. Foreign Direct Investment and the Domestic Capital Stock. *American Economic Review* 95, no. 2: 33–38.

Desai, Mihir A., C. Fritz Foley, and James R. Hines, Jr. 2009. Domestic Effects of the Foreign Activities of U.S. Multinationals. *American Economic Journal: Economic Policy* 1, no. 1: 181–203.

Devereux, Michael, and Rachel Griffith. 1999. *The Taxation of Discrete Investment Choices.* Working Paper Series no. W98/16. London: Institute for Fiscal Studies.

Dharmapala, Dhammika, C. Fritz Foley, and Kristin J. Forbes. 2011. Watch What I Do, Not What I Say: The Unintended Consequences of the Homeland Investment Act. *Journal of Finance* 66, no. 3: 753–87.

Doms, Mark E., and J. Bradford Jensen. 1998. Comparing Wages, Skills, and Productivity between Domestic and Foreign Owned Manufacturing Establishments in the United States. In *Geography and Ownership as Bases for Economic Accounting,* ed. Robert E. Baldwin, Robert E. Lipsey, and J. David Richardson. Chicago: University of Chicago Press for the National Bureau of Economic Research.

Ebenstein, Avraham, Ann Harrison, Margaret McMillan, and Shannon Phillips. 2009. *Estimating the Impact of Trade and Offshoring on American Workers Using the Current Population Surveys.* NBER Working Paper 15107. Cambridge, MA: National Bureau of Economic Research.

Edwards, Lawrence, and Robert Lawrence. 2013. *Rising Tide: Is Growth in Emerging Economies Good for the United States?* Washington: Peterson Institute for International Economics.

Faulkender, Michael, and Mitchell Petersen. 2009. *Investment and Capital Constraints: Repatriations under the American Jobs Creation Act.* NBER Working Paper 15248. Cambridge, MA: National Bureau of Economic Research.

Feenstra, Robert, and Gordon Hanson. 1999. The Impact of Outsourcing and High-Technology Capital on Wages: Estimates for the United States, 1979–1990. *Quarterly Journal of Economics* 114, no. 3: 907–40.

Geishecker, Ingo, Holger Gorg, and Daria Taglioni. 2009. Characterizing Euro Area Multinationals. *World Economy* 32, no. 1: 49–76.

Goldin, Claudia, and Larry Katz. 2008. *The Race between Education and Technology*. Cambridge, MA: Harvard University Press.

Govindarajan, Vijay, and Chris Trimble. 2012. *Innovation: Create Far From Home, Win Everywhere*. Boston, MA: Harvard Business School Press.

Grossman, G., and E. Rossi-Hansberg. 2008. Trading Tasks: A Simple Theory of Offshoring. *American Economic Review* 98, no. 5: 1978–97.

Grubert, Harry G. 2012. *Foreign Taxes and the Growing Share of U.S. Multinational Company Income Abroad: Profits, Not Sales, Are Being Globalized*. Office of Tax Analysis Working Paper 103. Washington: Office of Tax Analysis, Department of the Treasury.

Grubert, Harry G., and Rosanne Altshuler. 2012. Fixing the System: An Analysis of Alternative Proposals for the Reform of International Tax. Paper presented at the New Colloquium Series on Tax Policy and Public Finance, New York University, May 1.

Harrison, Ann, and Margaret McMillan. 2011. Offshoring Jobs? Multinationals and U.S. Manufacturing Employment. *Review of Economics and Statistics* 93, no. 3: 857–75.

Hassett, Kevin A., and Aparna Mathur. 2011. *Report Card on Effective Corporate Tax Rates: United States Gets an F* (February). Washington: American Enterprise Institute. Available at www.aei.org (accessed on March 9, 2011).

Head, Keith, and John Ries. 2001. Overseas Investment and Firm Exports. *Review of International Economics* 9, no 1: 108–22.

Hufbauer, Gary Clyde. 2012a. 800,000 Jobs Shipped Overseas? Check the Math! *Tax Notes* (August 6).

Hufbauer, Gary Clyde. 2012b. Rejoinder to Clausing. Letter to the editor. *Tax Analysts* (August 20).

Hufbauer, Gary Clyde, and Ariel Assa. 2007. *US Taxation of Foreign Income*. Washington: Peterson Institute for International Economics.

Hufbauer, Gary Clyde, and Dean DeRosa. 2010. Shortfalls in US Exports of Manufactured Goods. Unpublished draft. Peterson Institute for International Economics, Washington.

Hufbauer, Gary Clyde, and Paul Grieco. 2005. *Reforming the US Corporate Tax*. Washington: Institute for International Economics.

Hufbauer, Gary Clyde, assisted by Joanna M. van Rooij. 1992. *US Taxation of International Income: Blueprint for Reform*. Washington: Institute for International Economics.

Hufbauer, Gary Clyde, and Martin Vieiro. 2011. *US Tax Discrimination against Large Corporations Should Be Discarded*. Washington: Peterson Institute for International Economics.

Hufbauer, Gary Clyde, and Martin Vieiro. 2012a. *Right Idea, Wrong Direction: Obama's Corporate Tax Reform Proposals*. Policy Brief 12-13. Washington: Peterson Institute for International Economics.

Hufbauer, Gary Clyde, and Martin Vieiro. 2012b. How to Save Corporate Tax Reform: Stop Exaggerating the Revenue Cost. *Real Time Economic Issues Watch* (May 7). Washington: Peterson Institute for International Economics. Available at www.piie.com/blogs/realtime/?p=2863 (accessed on March 25, 2013).

Hufbauer, Gary Clyde, and Woan Foong Wong. 2011. *Corporate Tax Reform for a New Century*. Policy Brief 11-2. Washington: Peterson Institute for International Economics.

Hufbauer, Gary Clyde, Jeffrey J. Schott, and Woan Foong Wong. 2010. *Figuring Out the Doha Round*. Policy Analyses in International Economics 91. Washington: Peterson Institute for International Economics.

Jensen, J. Bradford. 2011. *Global Trade in Services: Fear, Facts, and Offshoring.* Washington: Peterson Institute for International Economics.

Jensen, J. Bradford, and Lori Kletzer. 2005. *Tradable Services: Understanding the Scope and Impact of Services Outsourcing.* Working Paper 05-9. Washington: Institute for International Economics.

Joint Committee on Taxation. 2011. Background and Selected Issues Related to the U.S. International Tax System and Systems That Exempt Foreign Business Income. JCX-33-11 (May 20). Washington.

JPMorgan. 2012. Global Tax Rate Makers. *North America Equity Research* (May 16). New York.

Kirkegaard, Jacob Funk. 2007. *The Accelerating Decline in America's High-Skilled Workforce: Implications for Immigration Policy.* Policy Analyses in International Economics 84. Washington: Peterson Institute for International Economics.

Kirkegaard, Jacob Funk. 2008. *Distance Isn't Quite Dead: Recent Trade Patterns and Modes of Supply in Computer and Information Services in the United States and NAFTA Partners.* Working Paper 08-10. Washington: Peterson Institute for International Economics.

Laffer, Arthur. 2004. *The Laffer Curve: Past, Present, and Future.* Heritage Foundation Backgrounder on Taxes 1765 (June 1). Available at www.heritage.org/research (accessed on March 25, 2013).

Leamer, Edward, and Michael Storper. 2001. The Economic Geography of the Internet Age. *Journal of International Business Studies* 32, no. 4: 641–65.

Levchenko, Andrei. 2007. Institutional Quality and International Trade. *Review of Economic Studies* 74, no. 3: 791–819.

Lipsey, Robert E., and Merle Yahr Weiss. 1981. Foreign Production and Exports in Manufacturing Industries. *Review of Economics and Statistics* 63, no. 4: 448–94.

Lipsey, Robert E., and Merle Yahr Weiss. 1984. Foreign Production and Exports of Individual Firms. *Review of Economics and Statistics* 66, no. 2: 304–08.

Lipsey, Robert E., Eric D. Ramstetter, and Magnus Blomström. 2000. *Outward FDI and Parent Exports and Employment: Japan, the United States, and Sweden.* NBER Working Paper 7623. Cambridge, MA: National Bureau of Economic Research.

Markusen, James R. 2006. Modeling the Offshoring of White-Collar Services: From Comparative Advantage to the New Theories of Trade and Foreign Direct Investment. In *Offshoring White-Collar Work,* ed. Lael Brainard and Susan M. Collins. Washington: Brookings Institution.

Markusen, James R., and Keith E. Maskus. 2003. General-Equilibrium Approaches to the Multinational Enterprise: A Review of Theory and Evidence. In *Handbook of International Trade,* ed. E. Kwan Choi and James Harrigan. London: Blackwell.

Mataloni, Raymond J., Jr., and Daniel R. Yorgason. 2002. Operations of U.S. Multinational Companies: Preliminary Results from the 1999 Benchmark Survey. *Survey of Current Business* (March): 24–54. Washington: Bureau of Economic Analysis.

McKinsey Global Institute. 2010. *Growth and Competitiveness in the United States: The Role of Its Multinational Companies.* Washington: McKinsey and Company.

Mertens, Karel, and Morten O. Ravn. 2011. *Corporate Income Tax Changes in the United States.* CEPR Discussion Paper 8554. London: Centre for Economic Policy Research. Available at www.cepr.org/pubs/new-dps/dplist.asp?dpno=8554.asp (accessed on March 25, 2013).

Mooij, Ruud A. de, and Sjef Ederveen. 2008. Corporate Tax Elasticities: A Reader's Guide to Empirical Findings. *Oxford Review of Economic Policy* 24, no 4: 680–97.

Moran, Theodore H., and Lindsay Oldenski. 2013. *Foreign Direct Investment in the United States: Benefits and Risks, with Special Attention to FDI from China.* Policy Analyses in International Economics 100. Washington: Peterson Institute for International Economics.

National Science Foundation. 2012. Research and Development: National Trends and International Comparisons. In *Science and Engineering Indicators 2012.* Available at www.nsf.gov/statistics/seind12/c4/c4s.htm (accessed on March 25, 2013).

Oberhofer, Harald, and Michael Pfaffermayr. 2012. FDI versus Exports: Multiple Host Countries and Empirical Evidence. *World Economy* 35, no. 3: 316–30.

OECD (Organization for Economic Cooperation and Development). 2008. *Tax Effects on Foreign Direct Investment: Recent Evidence and Policy Analysis.* OECD Tax Policy Study 17. Paris.

Oldenski, Lindsay. 2012. Export versus FDI and the Communication of Complex Information. *Journal of International Economics* 87, no. 2: 312–22.

Oler, Mitchell, Terry Shevlin, and Ryan Wilson. 2007. Examining Investor Expectations Concerning Tax Savings on the Repatriations of Foreign Earnings under the American Jobs Creation Act of 2004. *Journal of the American Taxation Association* 29, no. 2: 25–55.

Richardson, J. David. 2005a. Uneven Gains and Unbalanced Burdens? Three Decades of American Globalization. In *The United States and the World Economy,* ed. C. Fred Bergsten. Washington: Institute for International Economics.

Richardson, J. David. 2005b. Global Forces, American Faces: US Economic Globalization at the Grass Roots. Unpublished manuscript. Peterson Institute for International Economics, Washington.

Simpson, Helen. 2012. How Do Firms' Outward FDI Strategies Relate to Their Activity at Home? Empirical Evidence for the UK. *World Economy* 35, no. 3: 243–72.

Slaughter, Matthew J. 2010. *How US Multinational Companies Strengthen the US Economy: Revised Update.* Washington: US Council for International Business.

Slaughter, Matthew J., and Laura D'Andrea Tyson. 2012. A Warning Sign from Global Companies. *Harvard Business School Magazine* (March). Boston, MA: Harvard Business School.

Stephenson, Sherry, and Gary Hufbauer. 2011. Labor Mobility. In *Preferential Trade Agreement Policies for Development,* ed. Jean Pierre Chauffour and Jean Christoph Maur. Washington: World Bank.

Tyson, Laura D'Andrea, Kenneth Serwin, and Eric Drabkin. 2011. *The Benefits for the U.S. Economy of a Temporary Tax Reduction on the Repatriation of Foreign Subsidiary Earnings.* New America Foundation/Berkeley Research Group Working Paper (October 13). Available at www.newamerica. net/publications/policy/repatriation_tax_reduction (accessed on March 25, 2013).

World Bank, PwC, and IFC (World Bank, PriceWaterhouseCoopers, and International Finance Corporation). 2010. *Paying Taxes 2011: The Global Picture* (November 18). Available at www. pwc.com/payingtaxes (accessed on March 25, 2013).

Index

transfer pricing, 45
United Kingdom
  complementarity in, 23–24
  research and development facilities in, 33,
    37, 40
United States
  as competitive location, 1, 60
  deficits, 43, 49, 52–53
  economic role of MNCs in, 1, 3–11
  education quality, 61
  fear of FDI in, 2
  immigration system, 61–62

infrastructure, 62–63
US Bureau of Economic Analysis (BEA)
  surveys, 5, 13, 17, 22, 30–31
unit values of production, 15–16

visa programs, 61–62

wages, 7–8, 8t, 20–21, 23–25
World Trade Organization, 7

zero-sum view, of tax policy, 44

Other Publications from the
Peterson Institute for International Economics

WORKING PAPERS

94-1 APEC and Regional Trading Arrangements in the Pacific   Jeffrey A. Frankel with Shang-Jin Wei and Ernesto Stein

94-2 Towards an Asia Pacific Investment Code   Edward M. Graham

94-3 Merchandise Trade in the APEC Region: Is There Scope for Liberalization on an MFN Basis?   Paul Wonnacott

94-4 The Automotive Industry in Southeast Asia: Can Protection Be Made Less Costly?   Paul Wonnacott

94-5 Implications of Asian Economic Growth   Marcus Noland

95-1 APEC: The Bogor Declaration and the Path Ahead   C. Fred Bergsten

95-2 From Bogor to Miami…and Beyond: Regionalism in the Asia Pacific and the Western Hemisphere   Jeffrey J. Schott

95-3 Has Asian Export Performance Been Unique?   Marcus Noland

95-4 Association of Southeast Asian Nations and ASEAN Free Trade Area: Chronology and Statistics   Gautam Jaggi

95-5 The North Korean Economy   Marcus Noland

95-6 China and the International Economic System   Marcus Noland

96-1 APEC after Osaka: Toward Free Trade by 2010/2020   C. Fred Bergsten

96-2 Public Policy, Private Preferences, and the Japanese Trade Pattern   Marcus Noland

96-3 German Lessons for Korea: The Economics of Unification   Marcus Noland

96-4 Research and Development Activities and Trade Specialization in Japan   Marcus Noland

96-5 China's Economic Reforms: Chronology and Statistics   Gautam Jaggi, Mary Rundle, Daniel H. Rosen, and Yuichi Takahashi

96-6 US-China Economic Relations   Marcus Noland

96-7 The Market Structure Benefits of Trade and Investment Liberalization   Raymond Atje and Gary Clyde Hufbauer

96-8 The Future of US-Korea Economic Relations   Marcus Noland

96-9 Competition Policies in the Dynamic Industrializing Economies: The Case of China, Korea, and Chinese Taipei   Edward M. Graham

96-10 Modeling Economic Reform in North Korea   Marcus Noland, Sherman Robinson, and Monica Scatasta

96-11 Trade, Investment, and Economic Conflict Between the United States and Asia   Marcus Noland

96-12 APEC in 1996 and Beyond: The Subic Summit   C. Fred Bergsten

96-13 Some Unpleasant Arithmetic Concerning Unification   Marcus Noland

96-14 Restructuring Korea's Financial Sector for Greater Competitiveness   Marcus Noland

96-15 Competitive Liberalization and Global Free Trade: A Vision for the 21st Century   C. Fred Bergsten

97-1 Chasing Phantoms: The Political Economy of USTR   Marcus Noland

97-2 US-Japan Civil Aviation: Prospects for Progress   Jacqueline McFadyen

97-3 Open Regionalism   C. Fred Bergsten

97-4 Lessons from the Bundesbank on the Occasion of Its 40th (and Second to Last?) Birthday   Adam S. Posen

97-5 The Economics of Korean Unification   Marcus Noland, Sherman Robinson, and Li-Gang Liu

98-1 The Costs and Benefits of Korean Unification   Marcus Noland, Sherman Robinson, and Li-Gang Liu

98-2 Asian Competitive Devaluations   Li-Gang Liu, Marcus Noland, Sherman Robinson, and Zhi Wang

98-3 Fifty Years of the GATT/WTO: Lessons from the Past for Strategies or the Future   C. Fred Bergsten

98-4 NAFTA Supplemental Agreements: Four Year Review   Jacqueline McFadyen

98-5 Local Government Spending: Solving the Mystery of Japanese Fiscal Packages   Hiroko Ishii and Erika Wada

98-6 The Global Economic Effects of the Japanese Crisis   Marcus Noland, Sherman Robinson, and Zhi Wang

98-7 The Relationship Between Trade and Foreign Investment: Empirical Results for Taiwan and South Korea   Li-Gang Liu, The World Bank, and Edward M. Graham

99-1 Rigorous Speculation: The Collapse and Revival of the North Korean Economy   Marcus Noland, Sherman Robinson, and Tao Wang

99-2 Famine in North Korea: Causes and Cures   Marcus Noland, Sherman Robinson, and Tao Wang

99-3 Competition Policy and FDI: A Solution in Search of a Problem?   Marcus Noland

99-4 The Continuing Asian Financial Crisis: Global Adjustment and Trade   Marcus Noland, Sherman Robinson, and Zhi Wang

Economic Consequences of Soviet Disintegration* John Williamson, ed.
May 1993 ISBN 0-88132-190-7
Reconcilable Differences? United States-Japan Economic Conflict* C. Fred Bergsten and Marcus Noland
June 1993 ISBN 0-88132-129-X
Does Foreign Exchange Intervention Work? Kathryn M. Dominguez and Jeffrey A. Frankel
September 1993 ISBN 0-88132-104-4
Sizing Up U.S. Export Disincentives* J. David Richardson
September 1993 ISBN 0-88132-107-9
NAFTA: An Assessment Gary Clyde Hufbauer and Jeffrey J. Schott, rev. ed.
October 1993 ISBN 0-88132-199-0
Adjusting to Volatile Energy Prices Philip K. Verleger, Jr.
November 1993 ISBN 0-88132-069-2
The Political Economy of Policy Reform John Williamson, ed.
January 1994 ISBN 0-88132-195-8
Measuring the Costs of Protection in the United States Gary Clyde Hufbauer and Kimberly Ann Elliott
January 1994 ISBN 0-88132-108-7
The Dynamics of Korean Economic Development* Cho Soon
March 1994 ISBN 0-88132-162-1
Reviving the European Union* C. Randall Henning, Eduard Hochreiter, and Gary Clyde Hufbauer, eds.
April 1994 ISBN 0-88132-208-3
China in the World Economy Nicholas R. Lardy
April 1994 ISBN 0-88132-200-8
Greening the GATT: Trade, Environment, and the Future Daniel C. Esty
July 1994 ISBN 0-88132-205-9
Western Hemisphere Economic Integration* Gary Clyde Hufbauer and Jeffrey J. Schott
July 1994 ISBN 0-88132-159-1
Currencies and Politics in the United States, Germany, and Japan C. Randall Henning
September 1994 ISBN 0-88132-127-3
Estimating Equilibrium Exchange Rates John Williamson, ed.
September 1994 ISBN 0-88132-076-5
Managing the World Economy: Fifty Years after Bretton Woods Peter B. Kenen, ed.
September 1994 ISBN 0-88132-212-1
Reciprocity and Retaliation in U.S. Trade Policy Thomas O. Bayard and Kimberly Ann Elliott
September 1994 ISBN 0-88132-084-6
The Uruguay Round: An Assessment* Jeffrey J. Schott, assisted by Johanna Buurman
November 1994 ISBN 0-88132-206-7
Measuring the Costs of Protection in Japan* Yoko Sazanami, Shujiro Urata, and Hiroki Kawai
January 1995 ISBN 0-88132-211-3
Foreign Direct Investment in the United States, 3d ed. Edward M. Graham and Paul R. Krugman
January 1995 ISBN 0-88132-204-0
The Political Economy of Korea-United States Cooperation* C. Fred Bergsten and Il SaKong, eds.
February 1995 ISBN 0-88132-213-X

International Debt Reexamined* William R. Cline
February 1995 ISBN 0-88132-083-8
American Trade Politics, 3d ed. I. M. Destler
April 1995 ISBN 0-88132-215-6
Managing Official Export Credits: The Quest for a Global Regime* John E. Ray
July 1995 ISBN 0-88132-207-5
Asia Pacific Fusion: Japan's Role in APEC* Yoichi Funabashi
October 1995 ISBN 0-88132-224-5
Korea-United States Cooperation in the New World Order* C. Fred Bergsten and Il SaKong, eds.
February 1996 ISBN 0-88132-226-1
Why Exports Really Matter!* ISBN 0-88132-221-0
Why Exports Matter More!* ISBN 0-88132-229-6 J. David Richardson and Karin Rindal
July 1995; February 1996
Global Corporations and National Governments Edward M. Graham
May 1996 ISBN 0-88132-111-7
Global Economic Leadership and the Group of Seven C. Fred Bergsten and C. Randall Henning
May 1996 ISBN 0-88132-218-0
The Trading System after the Uruguay Round* John Whalley and Colleen Hamilton
July 1996 ISBN 0-88132-131-1
Private Capital Flows to Emerging Markets after the Mexican Crisis* Guillermo A. Calvo, Morris Goldstein, and Eduard Hochreiter
September 1996 ISBN 0-88132-232-6
The Crawling Band as an Exchange Rate Regime: Lessons from Chile, Colombia, and Israel John Williamson
September 1996 ISBN 0-88132-231-8
Flying High: Liberalizing Civil Aviation in the Asia Pacific* Gary Clyde Hufbauer and Christopher Findlay
November 1996 ISBN 0-88132-227-X
Measuring the Costs of Visible Protection in Korea* Namdoo Kim
November 1996 ISBN 0-88132-236-9
The World Trading System: Challenges Ahead Jeffrey J. Schott
December 1996 ISBN 0-88132-235-0
Has Globalization Gone Too Far? Dani Rodrik
March 1997 ISBN paper 0-88132-241-5
Korea-United States Economic Relationship* C. Fred Bergsten and Il SaKong, eds.
March 1997 ISBN 0-88132-240-7
Summitry in the Americas: A Progress Report Richard E. Feinberg
April 1997 ISBN 0-88132-242-3
Corruption and the Global Economy Kimberly Ann Elliott
June 1997 ISBN 0-88132-233-4
Regional Trading Blocs in the World Economic System Jeffrey A. Frankel
October 1997 ISBN 0-88132-202-4
Sustaining the Asia Pacific Miracle: Environmental Protection and Economic Integration Andre Dua and Daniel C. Esty
October 1997 ISBN 0-88132-250-4

Australia, New Zealand,
and Papua New Guinea
D. A. Information Services
648 Whitehorse Road
Mitcham, Victoria 3132, Australia
Tel: 61-3-9210-7777
Fax: 61-3-9210-7788
Email: service@dadirect.com.au
www.dadirect.com.au

India, Bangladesh, Nepal, and Sri Lanka
Viva Books Private Limited
Mr. Vinod Vasishtha
4737/23 Ansari Road
Daryaganj, New Delhi 110002
India
Tel: 91-11-4224-2200
Fax: 91-11-4224-2240
Email: viva@vivagroupindia.net
www.vivagroupindia.com

Mexico, Central America, South America,
and Puerto Rico
US PubRep, Inc.
311 Dean Drive
Rockville, MD 20851
Tel: 301-838-9276
Fax: 301-838-9278
Email: c.falk@ieee.org

Asia *(Brunei, Burma, Cambodia, China,*
Hong Kong, Indonesia, Korea, Laos, Malaysia,
Philippines, Singapore, Taiwan, Thailand,
and Vietnam)
East-West Export Books (EWEB)
University of Hawaii Press
2840 Kolowalu Street
Honolulu, Hawaii 96822-1888
Tel: 808-956-8830
Fax: 808-988-6052
Email: eweb@hawaii.edu

Canada
Renouf Bookstore
5369 Canotek Road, Unit 1
Ottawa, Ontario KIJ 9J3, Canada
Tel: 613-745-2665
Fax: 613-745-7660
www.renoufbooks.com

Japan
United Publishers Services Ltd.
1-32-5, Higashi-shinagawa
Shinagawa-ku, Tokyo 140-0002
Japan
Tel: 81-3-5479-7251
Fax: 81-3-5479-7307
Email: purchasing@ups.co.jp
For trade accounts only. Individuals will find
Institute books in leading Tokyo bookstores.

Middle East
MERIC
2 Bahgat Ali Street, El Masry Towers
Tower D, Apt. 24
Zamalek, Cairo
Egypt
Tel. 20-2-7633824
Fax: 20-2-7369355
Email: mahmoud_fouda@mericonline.com
www.mericonline.com

United Kingdom, Europe
***(including Russia and Turkey)*, Africa,**
and Israel
The Eurospan Group
c/o Turpin Distribution
Pegasus Drive
Stratton Business Park
Biggleswade, Bedfordshire
SG18 8TQ
United Kingdom
Tel: 44 (0) 1767-604972
Fax: 44 (0) 1767-601640
Email: eurospan@turpin-distribution.com
www.eurospangroup.com/bookstore

Visit our website at:
www.piie.com
E-mail orders to:
petersonmail@presswarehouse.com